curiosamente

VIVAVENICE

ELZEVIRO

C'è una città di questo mondo,
ma così bella, ma così strana,
che pare un gioco di fata Morgana
o una visione del cuore profondo.
Avviluppata in un roseo velo,
sta con sue chiese, palazzi, giardini,
tutta sospesa tra due turchini,
quello del mare, quello del cielo...

Diego Valeri

There is a city in this world,
so beautiful, so strange,
it looks like a mirage
or a vision from the deepest heart.
Enveloped in a pink veil,
it lies with its churches, palaces and gardens,
all suspended between two cobalt blues,
the one of the sea, the one of the sky...

Diego Valeri

Paola Zoffoli - Paola Scibilia

VIVAVENICE

a guide to exploring, learning and having fun

ELZEVIRO

VIVAVENICE
*A guide to exploring, learning
and having fun*

© Elzeviro - English edition 2005

The editorial concept, the title and the sub-title constitute
an integral part of the series *Curiosamente* and are the
exclusive property of the publisher.

Graphic coordination and editorial direction
Alessandro Tusset

Written by
Paola Zoffoli © 1998

Translated by
Susan Maggioni

Illustrations by
Paola Scibilia © 1998

Graphic Art consultant
Scibilia&Scibilia

Editing consultant
Olga Barmine

Printed by
Centrooffset Master

ELZEVIRO EDITIONS
via Armando Diaz 20, Treviso
web-site: *www.elzeviro.com*
e-mail: *info@elzeviro.com*

ISBN 88-87528-04-7

*Our heartfelt thanks go to Guido Lion
(for historical assistance and help in the
complex work of revising the text),
Fabrizia Maschietto (for her kind assistance),
Michelle Lovric (for her precious advice) and
Gianfranco Vianello (a real 'Venexian', who
was happy to share with us the oddities and
secrets of this extraordinary city).
We would like to express our gratitude to the
children of Venice who have co-operated
and eagerly participated in the interviews in
preparation of the chapter "Venice a place to
play", without forgetting all the other people
who have helped us in this absorbing job.
We would, finally, like to thank Venice,
a magical and fascinating city, with which
we have always been deeply in love.*

This guide is dedicated to
Giulia, Matteo, Sonam Gyatso,
Andrea, Jacopo, Eric and to
everyone who loves Venice.

Summary

Preface

There is no place in the world which is better able than Venice to express the idea of a fantastic voyage in search of a city's secrets. Seemingly suspended between earth and sky, in a dimension of dreams where time almost stands still, Venice is there, a glorious witness to the magnificence of its long history: the history of a city brilliantly "stolen" from the sea and which drew from the sea the energy it needed to become a symbol of timeless beauty.

This is why we felt it to be our duty to dedicate this guide to Venice: a detailed "map" which will lead you on a kind of "treasure hunt"… this is what it's really for!

The richly illustrated pages of this book are ready to reveal all the secrets of Venice past and present, about the myths, the legends, the popular traditions, the great men and events which made her so famous. And in addition to the classic itineraries to visit churches, palaces and museums, with a little fantasy it will introduce you to the magic of a different Venice: the Venice of labyrinths, the intricate web of tortuous little streets where you get lost and found again, where walking as you are peacefully lulled by the sound of the water or the loud local dialect can be a vacation in and of itself.

Hour after hour, from sunrise to sunset, there are a thousand different Venices to light up the eyes of its visitors, because there are a thousand different kinds of light which envelope this mysterious floating city. And so, as you discover this overwhelming richness(often hidden to the distracted tourist) or simply abandon yourself to the feelings in your soul, this guide will be a faithful travel companion to you: it will help you to grasp the most curious and fascinating aspects of this enchanted city, connecting them all, like a game, into a more complete,profound and original picture in a memory that will last forever.

Alessandro Tusset

11

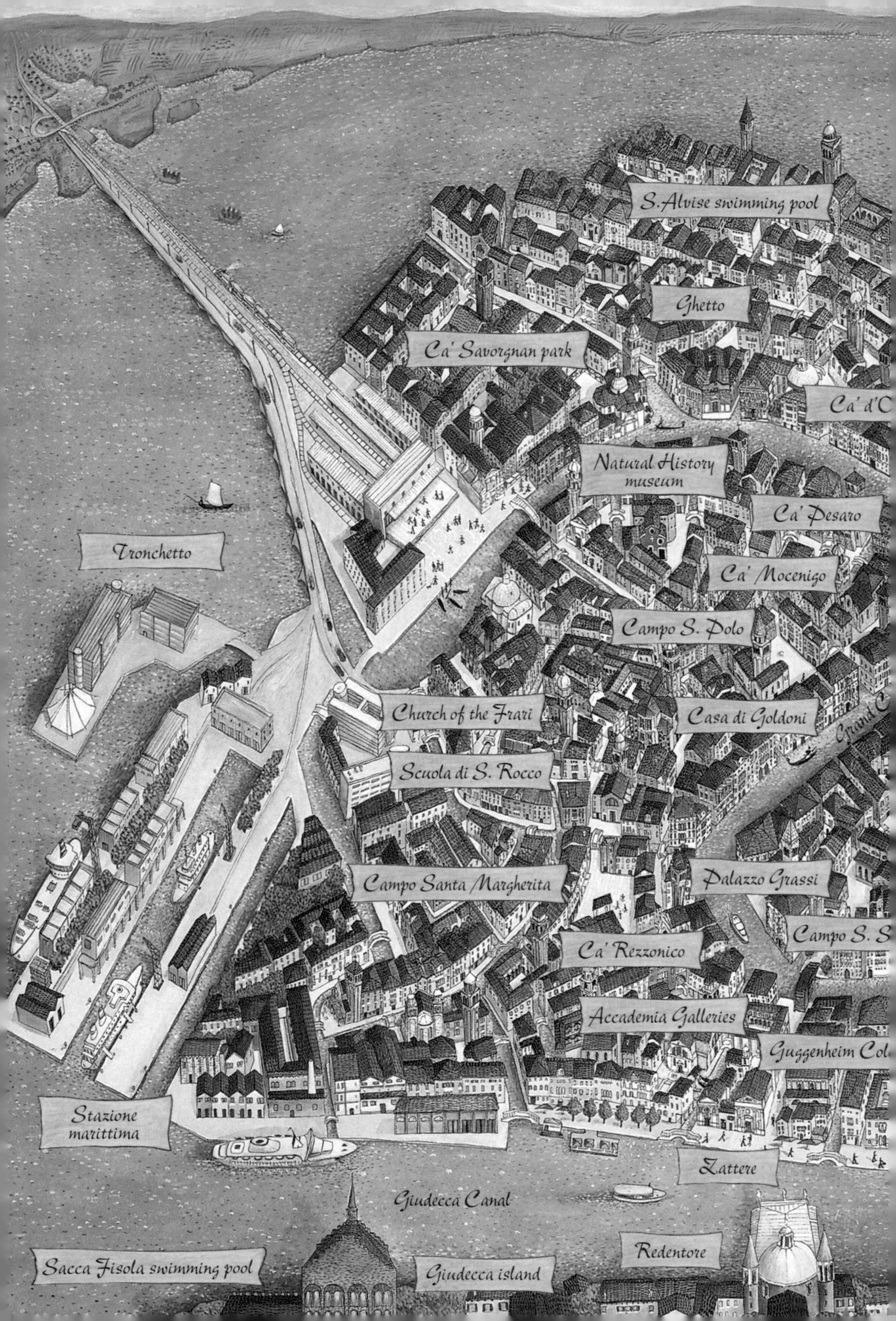

S. Alvise swimming pool

Ghetto

Ca' Savorgnan park

Ca' d'C

Natural History museum

Ca' Pesaro

Ca' Mocenigo

Tronchetto

Campo S. Polo

Church of the Frari

Casa di Goldoni

Scuola di S. Rocco

Grand C

Campo Santa Margherita

Palazzo Grassi

Campo S. S

Ca' Rezzonico

Accademia Galleries

Guggenheim Col

Stazione marittima

Zattere

Giudecca Canal

Sacca Fisola swimming pool

Giudecca island

Redentore

Murano

San Michele

Venezia

Torcello and Burano →

San Zanipolo

Church of Miracles

Scuola di San Giorgio degli Sc.

Rialto

Querini Stampalia

S.M. Formosa

Arsenale

San Marco

Church of the Pietà

S. Pietro di Castello

Correr museum

Riva degli Schiavoni

Museum of Naval History

Chiesa della Salute

Biennale gardens

S. Elena gardens

San Giorgio

Lido →

History

The lion of St. Mark
The birth of the city
The Serenissima Republic
Venice today
Living in Venice

The lion of St. Mark

Venice and lions

The **winged lion** is surely the image you will see most often in Venice; while exploring the city and walking trough at *campi* (squares) and *campielli* (small squares) you will run into lots of them. ⌒ p. 29-30

In *Piazza San Marco* alone there are at least fourteen. In the **Piazzetta dei Leoncini**, next to the *Basilica di San Marco* ⌒ p. 82-83, there are two of them, very popular with younger children who are always asking to have rides on them. Can you find out where the others are?

To see a whole band of lion statues, as many as four, all you have to do is go to the *Arsenale*, a place where Venetians used to build and repair the Republic's ships, which is today a military area. ⌒ p. 99

The two bigger lions which guard the entrance were taken as war loot from the Piraeus, Athens harbour.

The gonfalon of Venice
It is the Serenissima Republic's flag:
it pictures the winged lion, symbol of
the city, drawn in gold on a dark red
background.

The winged lion

It is pictured with an open Book of Gospels carrying the inscription PAX TIBI MARCE EVANGELISTA MEUS (Peace to you, Mark, my Evangelist).

According to legend, an angel said these words to St. Mark while he was preaching on the islands of the lagoon, to prophesy the peace of eternal rest which the Evangelist would have found in the lagoon city. The saint's body is, in fact, still buried in Venice, inside the Basilica di San Marco. ⌒ p. 82-83

St. Mark

St. Theodore was Venice's patron saint at the beginning of its history, but the Venetians later chose St. Mark to protect and represent their city, which was growing in power and wealth. For this reason the two Venetian merchants *Rustego* and *Bon* smuggled the Saint's remains from *Alexandria in Egypt* in the 9th century.

According to legend, to avoid Muslim inspection the Saint's body was covered with pieces of pork, a forbidden food for Muslims. With this stratagem it was safely taken to Venice, and here laid to rest in the Basilica. The winged lion, symbol of *Mark the Evangelist*, has since then become the city's emblem; the beautiful church in Piazza San Marco was dedicated to the saint. Two columns standing in front of the *Bacino di San Marco* are topped by *St. Theodore* and the winged lion. ⌒ p. 90

War lion

In war times, the lion was pictured with book closed and a sword in its paw to defend the city, symbolizing the Serenissima Republic's military might.

The birth of the city

421 A.D. According to tradition, Venice is founded on the 25th of March.

450-453 A.D. The start of Barbarian invasions in Northern Italy.

570 A.D. Some refugees from cities in the Veneto region (North-East Italy) settle on the lagoon islands to flee the invading Barbarians.

639 A.D. One of the first settlements is on the island of *Torcello*, where the *Bishop of Altino* seeks refuge with a group of refugees and founds the *cathedral.* ↷ p. 118 Initially the community is under the protection of an Imperial Officer of Byzantium.

697 A.D. The first local *Dux* (Latin for leader, *Doge* in Venetian) is elected. According to legend, his name is *Paoluccio Anafesto.* ↷ p. 90

8ᵗʰ century A.D. The centre of Byzantine power moves from *Eraclea* to *Malamocco*, on the *Lido* island. ↷ p. 115 Commercial contacts with Adriatic Sea ports strengthen, thanks to the lagoon city's strategic position in the salt trade.

810 A.D. The doge elected in Malamocco moves to the centre of the lagoon, in the *Rivo Alto* area (the islands around *Rialto* ↷ p. 92).

814 A.D. Construction of the first Doge's palace begins. ↷ p. 87

828 A.D. Two Venetian merchants smuggle the body of Saint Mark from Alexandria in Egypt. ↷ p. 17
The winged lion becomes the city's symbol, to establish its religious and political independence from Byzantium.

1000 A.D. The first *Sensa* p. 111, the wedding with the sea, is officiated to mark the victory of the *Doge Pietro Orseolo II* against the Adriatic Sea pirates. Venice's economic and political power grows thanks to commercial exchanges. It is now ready to conquer the Eastern Mediterranean Sea: the *Serenissima Republic* is born.

Let's play together

Discover what's hidden in the picture

Use your favorite color to fill in the areas with a dot.

The Serenissima Republic

Strategic Position

With the Crusades the Serenissima Republic managed to establish bases for its trade in the East, to strengthen its hold on the Mediterranean basin.

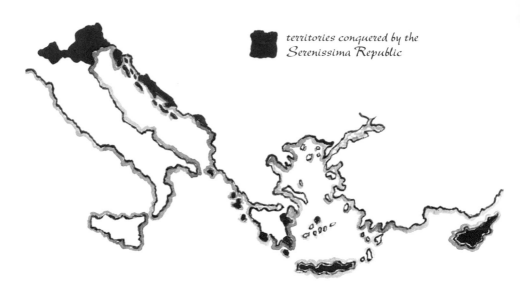

territories conquered by the
Serenissima Republic

Diplomacy

Venice soon became so politically powerful that in 1177 the Doge *Ziani* acted as mediator to bring about the reconciliation between *Frederick Barbarossa*, emperor of the Holy Roman Empire, and Pope *Alessandro III*.

Shrewdness

The Serenissima exploited the *4ᵗʰ Crusade* to beat Byzantium; in exchange for the fleet it supplied, the *Doge Enrico Dandolo* ⌐ p. 90 convinced the other crusaders to lay siege to Constantinople, which was conquered in 1204. The victory gave the Venetians important commercial privileges.

The oligarchic political system

The government system on which the Republic was based lasted for over one thousand years. Apart from the Doge, whose powers were limited by the *Venetian Constitution*, there was the *Consiglio dei Dieci* (the Council of Ten), which tried crimes against the State, and the *Maggior Consiglio*, which consisted of approximately two thousand members of noble families, registered in the *Libro d'Oro* (Golden Book), whose task was to elect the Doge and the other magistrates. This system is defined "oligarchy", a Greek-origin word which means government of the few. ⌐ p. 89

Marco Polo: the incredible journey of a Venetian merchant

In 1261 the young *Marco Polo*, who was born near Rialto ⌐ p. 92 in the **Corte del Milion** set off for China with his father *Nicolò* and his uncle *Matteo*. After a four-year journey the three Venetian merchants reached *Cambaluc*, the present-day Beijing. They were welcomed with great honours, and spent over twenty years at the Kublai Khan's court. During his stay in China Marco Polo became a friend of the *Great Khan*, and was appointed diplomat. He took a great interest in the production of sugar, spices, silk and cotton, which were particularly precious products for the West. When he went back to Italy, (he brought spaghetti back!) he was taken prisoner by the Genoese. While in prison, he dictated his memoirs in French to his prison mate *Rustichello da Pisa*. This was how the famous *Il Milion* (*The Travels of Marco Polo*) was written.

Caterina Cornaro: the beautiful queen of Cyprus

In the 15th century the Serenissima wanted to conquer the island of Cyprus. *Caterina Cornaro*, who was from a noble Venetian family, married *Giacomo II of Lusignano*, king of Cyprus. Just one year later, Caterina was expecting a baby and was a widow: legend has it that the new born heir to the throne was poisoned by the Venetians, who wanted to rule the island. Caterina was enthroned and reigned until 1489, when she was called back to Venice. She was received with the honours reserved only to great sovereigns. She gave Cyprus over to the Serenissima, obtaining the fiefdom of Asolo, near Treviso, in exchange.

The *Historical Regatta* takes place on the Grand Canal to the present day to commemorate these events. ʌ p. 63

The Unconquerable City

In the 15th and 16th centuries Venice became a great power: it had conquered the North East of Italy (*Stato da tera*, land state) and, after neutralizing the Sea Republic of Genoa, had the monopoly of trade in the Adriatic Sea – which was also called "the Venetian Gulf" – and in the Mediterranean (*Stato da mar*, sea state).

Built for the most part in wood, the city grew and expanded rapidly.

The *Arsenale* shipyard worked non-stop to build and improve the fleet. ʌ p. 99

Wood thus became a crucial strategic resource for the Serenissima's survival; initially it came from the forests of the Venetian mainland such as Cansiglio and Montello; later, because of impoverished resources, from Cadore, Istria and Dalmatia.

Wood was also used to make *bricole* ʌ p. 49, the huge poles that mark the waterways of the lagoon canals. Venetians only had to remove these signals for any enemy ship to get stuck in the shallow waters of the lagoon, becoming an easy prey; the city could not be attacked by its enemies.

The fight against the Turks and the decline

In addition to the danger represented by the *League of Cambrai* (1508) which wanted to destroy the Serenissima, Venice had to deal with the Turks who conquered various possessions, and were in continuous expansion. The victory of the Venetian fleet over the Turks in 1571 at *Lepanto* (in Western Greece) was not decisive and Venice continued to lose part of its territories. In the 17th century the Serenissima was in crisis; it suffered two catastrophic outbreaks of the Black Death p. 79 and lost monopoly over sea trade, which moved to the North Sea and the Americas.

As a consequence the great sea Republic started to decline and, with Napoleon's invasion in 1797, it ceased to exist forever. p. 40

Let's play together

Marco Polo's route

Join the dots and you will find the route Marco Polo followed during the journey he described in the book *Il Milion*.

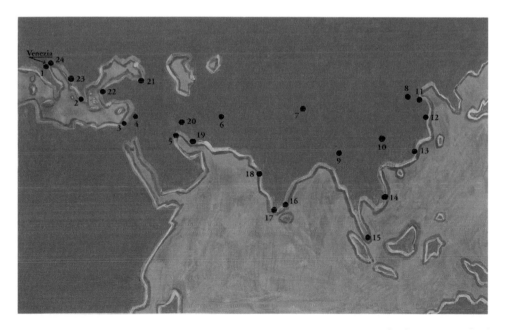

Venice Today

Venice is the chief provincial and regional town. At present its number of inhabitants has fallen considerably, both due to the high cost of houses (many of which belong to foreigners, who only use them a couple of weeks a year) and the difficulty of finding work. Today there are only 70,000 residents (in 1950 there were 150,000), as opposed to 240,000 in Mestre. Every year, approximately 2,000 residents move out of Venice. This phenomenon has caused the population to age: today the average age is around 50. Unlike other Italian cities, you won't see many children around; schools and kindergartens have ever lower attendance numbers. Young couples tend, in fact, to move to the *terraferma* , the word Venetians use to describe not only the city of *Mestre* (which forms one single municipality with Venice), but all the rest of the territory which lies beyond the **Ponte della Libertà**.

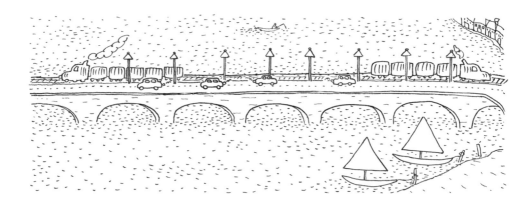

The bridge, which originally had only railway tracks (1846), and only much later (1932) a road too, has completely revolutionized Venice's position: the city which used to be isolated and could only be reached by water, is now connected to the *terraferma*. The **Marco Polo airport** in Tessera (13 km from Venice) connects the city to the rest of the world. Those who arrive by car must leave it in a **parking area** on **Tronchetto** island or at **Piazzale Roma**. You can only enter Venice on foot or by boat!

The economy

The development and economic wealth of Venice have always been related to its special geographical condition of a lagoon city. Fishing and sea trading are the most traditional activities.

Shipbuilding and port activities represent another aspect of the city's economic resources, especially since the new harbour has been built to dock the large cruise ships which call here.

Industrial development is concentrated in the **Porto Marghera** area and constitutes an important part of the Venetian economy. The most productive sectors are chemicals, mechanics and metal working. Local agriculture specializes in fruit and vegetables, which are mainly grown on the lagoon islands, like *Le Vignole* and *Sant'Erasmo* (called the *vegetable garden of Venice*). ↷ p. 113

All arts and crafts are also important; glass making, lace making, masks, marble paper and luxury textiles, but also gilding and furniture restoration, book binding and jewellery. ↷ p. 64
But the main source of wealth today is **tourism:** each year there are more than 12 million visitors. This crucial sector of the Venetian economy means jobs in hotels and restaurants; co-operatives of motorboat pilots and gondoliers; tourist agencies and shops.

Living in Venice

Living in Venice means living in a magical, really special place. It is a city built on water: so there are no cars, motorbikes or mopeds. No bicycles either, since to be able to cross the innumerable bridges you would end up having to carry it all the time: steps and wheels don't go well together at all! Walking among people offers many opportunities for social life: you go out to buy the bread and inevitably run into someone you know, so you stop for a chat without the hassle of parking the car, and you learn to take things easy. In this respect Venice has a much more human and relaxed rhythm than other cities.

You will probably see Venetians pulling small carts full of groceries over bridges. This city teaches you to take your strength into due account: you'll have to carry everything you need with your own arms, so people are much more careful not to buy useless things. Moreover, there are no hyper-markets or shopping malls: instead, there are small shops where for space reasons, the choice of goods on display is restricted to essential items. You will hear people speak in dialect everywhere: the *venexian* ↷ p. 135 is the language that distinguishes Venetians from the "foresti" (the non-Venetians) and it is still largely spoken among all social classes.

What about the internet?

If you are a computer buff and you are interested in finding other useful information, look for it at these addresses:

www.virtualvenice.net
www.venetia.it
www.venetianlegends.it

 # Oddities

How many bridges are there in Venice?

416 bridges connecting 118 lagoon islands across approximately 200 canals.

What were the "Scuole Grandi"?

They were not real schools, but great guilds of people doing the same job, and also charities which assisted the poor, as well as religious brotherhoods. Apart from various minor Scuole, there used to be six *Scuole Grandi* in Venice, each one of them with their own patron saint: *Santa Maria della Misericordia, Santa Maria della Carità, San Giovanni Evangelista, San Marco, San Rocco* p. 95 and *San Teodoro*.

What does ciao mean?

It comes from the Venetian *s'ciavo vostro* (your servant), a courtesy expression with which people used to greet each other.

What are "cicheti"?

They are little savoury snacks eaten in the *bàcari* (small, typical Venetian pubs) made with meat (like meat balls), vegetables (grilled or sautéed) and fish (like cod tartines, fried fish kebabs or *sarde in saor*, i.e. marinated with onions, pine seeds and raisins, an ancient Venetian method for preserving food).

Has the lagoon ever frozen?

Yes, more than once in particularly cold winters, such as in 1708, when Venetians were able to reach the *terraferma* on foot for the first time. The *Ponte della Libertà* and the *railway* had not been built yet, and Venice could only be reached by sea. It happened again, more recently, in 1929.

Architecture

Did you know that...
How Venice was built
The Grand Canal
Palace styles
Window styles
The Venetian palazzo

Did you know that...

Rio
The name of canals, which cross the city like many water roads.

Fondamenta
It is the street that runs along the banks of a canal.

Campo
The name of Venetian squares, which used to be covered with grass.

Calle
The road, street or alley of Venice.

The well-curb
In carved stone, it is the visible part of a complex system of drinking water supply.

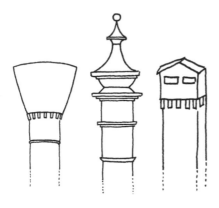

Calletta is a narrow lane, much smaller than the calle.

Fumaiolo is the chimney pot. It generally has the shape of a truncated upside-down cone, like the funnel of an engine. It can also look like a helmet, a top hat, a cube or an obelisk.

Campiello is a smaller square than the campo.

Ramo is a short side alley, often a blind alley.

Riva flanks the lagoon or canal and it is a paved edge onto which boats can be moored.

Sottoportego is a short covered passage under a building.

Salizada indicates an important street and used to be paved, unlike the calle, with silica stone slabs.

Ruga derives from the French *rue* (street) and indicates a calle with many shops.

Corte is a sort of small courtyard shared by several houses.

Rio terà is a canal which was closed and filled in later to become a street.

Piscina was a marsh with stagnant water, which is today filled up with earth.

Stazio is the landing where gondolas stop.

Under the well curb there is a tank filled with sand, which was used to filter rain water.

Altana is the typical Venetian wooden terrace, built like a nest on the roof of a house.

Campanile: a bell tower, almost always square based, was used as a sighting tower. Sometimes there is a beautiful clock on its front.

Sestiere is one of the six districts into which Venice is divided; *Castello, San Marco, Cannaregio, Dorsoduro, San Polo* and *Santa Croce.*

■ **Cannaregio**
■ **San Marco**
■ **Santa Croce**
■ **Castello**
■ **Dorsoduro**
■ **San Polo**

The address of a Venetian house, unlike any other city, has the name of the sestiere and the house number, not a street name. House numbers – which are therefore progressive, grouped in sestiere – can be very high, often higher than six thousand.

Help! I got lost in the maze of Venetian streets!
The intricate web of calli and callette is so entangled, that getting lost is absolutely normal; Venetians are used to giving information to baffled tourists who have lost their way. If the map looks incomprehensible and you no longer know where you are, do not give up hope: you will find someone to direct you.

How Venice was built

Venice was built on the thin strips of land which form the lagoon islands. People have always found ingenious solutions to the problem of building structures on water that are elastic and not too heavy. This explains the extensive use of loggias and arches to 'empty' and lighten up the buildings, but especially the particular con-

Caranto

It is deep and constitutes a solid foundation for buildings. It is formed by alternate layers of sand and clay.

In contact with the *caranto*, the wooden poles driven into the ground tend, with time, to harden, creating a solid base for the foundations.

The foundations

To make the soil firmer, larch or fir poles are driven into the soil. Even if they are submerged, they do not rot because of the lack of oxygen. The *zattaron* is then laid (a kind of platform made of two wooden planks cemented with a mixture of stone and bricks) which is sealed with foundations in Istria stone, a kind of water-proof marble.

struction method used. This craft was learnt more than one thousand years ago, when it was discovered that the wood from the Serenissima larch forests, once submerged in clay and in contact with salt water, became as hard as stone.

The brickwork

At this point the real masonry is done. The floor base is built in wooden beams covered with planks, on which the floor, called *terrazzo*, is laid.

This is made of a mixture of lime and bits of stone, brick and coloured marble, beaten until the surface is smooth.

The plaster

The front can be faced with bricks or be plastered.

It is often covered with a brick-red plaster, called *coccio pesto*, which is obtained by crushing and mixing bits of bricks and roof tiles with mortar.

The Grand Canal

Venice has the shape of a fish cut in half by the Grand Canal. This big snake is about 4.2 kilometres long and between 3 and 5 metres deep. It divides the city in two parts: on one side the sestieri of Dorsoduro, San Polo and Santa Croce, on the other side Cannaregio, Castello and San Marco. It has only four big bridges crossing it.

"The fourth bridge" over the Grand Canal was designed by the Spanish architect *Santiago Calatrava*. It connects the train station to *Piazzale Roma* along a modern arched walkway made of glass, steel and panels of Istria stone.

Ponte degli Scalzi takes its name from the *church of the Scalzi* nearby, which was built by the *Carmelite friars,* who even in winter used to wear sandals with no socks (*scalzi* means barefoot in Italian).

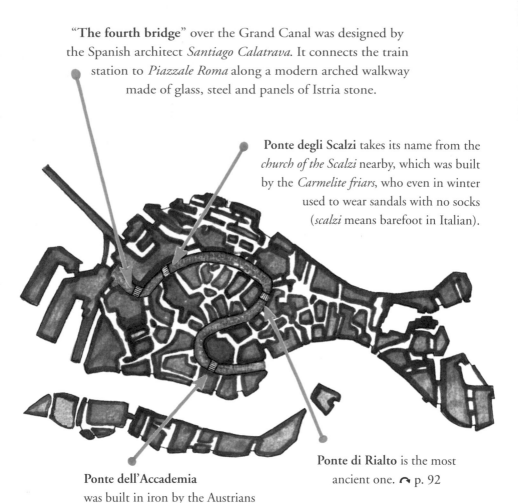

Ponte dell'Accademia was built in iron by the Austrians in the 1800's and later rebuilt in wood.

Ponte di Rialto is the most ancient one. ↷ p. 92

Cruising by gondola or water bus down the *Canal Grande*, which the Venetians affectionately call the *Canalazzo*, you will be able to admire the magnificent palaces on this wide thoroughfare. You will see the most important buildings built between the 13th and the 18th century that belonged to great noble families, whose names still indicate the palaces today: *Vendramin, Tron, Michiel, Venier, Foscari, Corner, Grimani, Barbarigo, Contarini, Pisani, Pesaro* and many more. All the palaces face the Grand Canal, and their main façade is often decorated with arches, loggias, coloured marble and wide windows.

Today some of these buildings have become the seat of public offices (such as *Palazzo Balbi*, where the Veneto Regional Council has its seat), museums, (such as *Ca' Rezzonico*, seat of the Museum of 18th century Venice) ↷ p.105 or Universities (like *Ca' Foscari*).

Palazzo Grassi
Recently restored, it is today a centre for prestigious art exhibitions.
telephone 041 5231680
Water bus San Samuele

Palace styles

The most ancient palaces like *Ca' Farsetti* or *Ca' Loredan* were built in the **Venetian-Byzantine style** (13th century). They have the *fondaco* structure, which are houses with a *loggia* on the first floor and a *portico* on the ground floor for storing goods. ⌒ p. 67

Ca' Farsetti

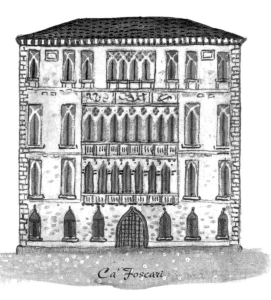

Ca' Foscari

The palaces built in the **Gothic style** (14th - mid 15th century) like *Palazzo Ducale, Ca' Foscari, Palazzo Pisani Moretta* or *Ca' d'Oro*, display refined and precious decorations which look like elegant lace.

In the palaces of the **Renaissance style** (15th and 16th century), like *Ca' Grimani* or *Ca' Vendramin Calergi* (today the seat of the Casinò), the façades are inspired by the classical ancient Greek and Roman style, both in shape and harmonious proportions.

Ca' Vendramin Calergi

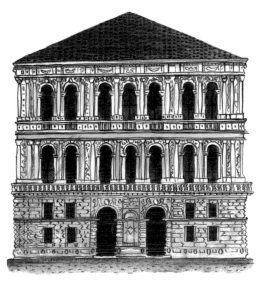

Ca' Pesaro

With the triumph of the **Baroque style** (17th century), palaces were built with an eye for scenic effects such as *Ca'Rezzonico* or *Ca'Pesaro*: on the façade, decorated with *mascheroni* ⌒ p. 147, the play of light and shade is accentuated.

Window styles

The windows of Venetian palaces are divided by small columns and can be:
bifore (with two arches)
trifore (with three arches)
polifore (with many arches).

Three-arched window

Many-arched gothic window

Gothic style windows are often decorated with floral motifs and have the traditional acute arch shape, pointed at the top.

The most ancient windows are in the **Venetian-Byzantine style** and you can recognise them because the arches have a special shape, called "horseshoe".

Two-arched window

To increase the light-shade effect, windows of the baroque period are richly decorated with groups of columns, garlands, cherubs and mascheroni. ↻ p. 147

With the advent of the **Renaissance style**, window arches become semicircular.

The Venetian palazzo

The Venetian palace had three functions:
public, as it was representative of the noble family that lived in it;
commercial, for the trade and business that was carried out on the ground floor;
residential, since the family and its servants lived there.

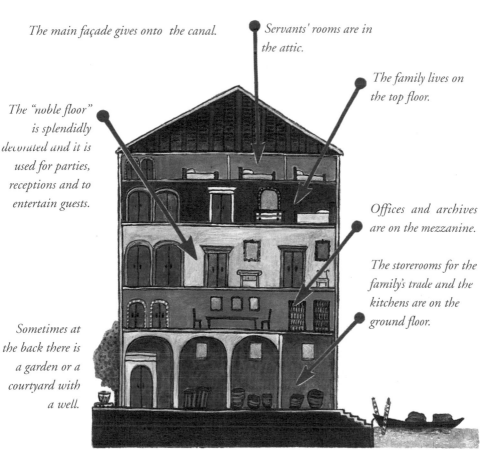

The main façade gives onto the canal.

Servants' rooms are in the attic.

The "noble floor" is splendidly decorated and it is used for parties, receptions and to entertain guests.

The family lives on the top floor.

Offices and archives are on the mezzanine.

The storerooms for the family's trade and the kitchens are on the ground floor.

Sometimes at the back there is a garden or a courtyard with a well.

Access from the canal is through the "water door".

Oddities

Who said the famous sentence I shall be like Attila in Venice?

Napoleon Bonaparte, before declaring war and invading Venice on the 1st of May, 1797. The French general then handed the city over to his Austrian allies. Many Venetian patriots (such as *Daniele Manin* and *Nicolò Tommaseo*), followers of *Risorgimento* revolutionary ideas, later rebelled against them. Only in 1866 did Venice finally free itself from Austrian domination and join the Kingdom of Italy.

How many university colleges are there in Venice today?

Five: Foreign Languages and Literature; Literature and Philosophy; Mathematics, Physics and Natural Sciences; Economics and Business Administration; Architecture.

What are tramezzini?

They are triangular sandwiches made with soft bread (the kind used for toasted sandwiches), spread with mayonnaise and with different fillings: vegetables (such as spinach or tomatoes), mushrooms, ham, boiled eggs, cheese or fish (such as tuna or shrimps).

Who was the "codega"?

A servant who accompanied the noble men disguised with *bauta*  p. 79 at night, guiding them with a lantern.

What is the meaning of Mercerie and Frezzeria, two important streets near Piazza San Marco?

Haberdashers', perfumeries and pharmacists' shops used to be in the *Mercerie*, while, in the Middle Ages, people used to buy arrows (*frecce* in Italian) in the *Frezzeria*.

Who was Carlo Scarpa?

He was a famous Venetian architect who managed to restore buildings without destroying or altering the spirit of the lagoon city.
If you are interested in seeing how the ancient and the new can co-exist harmo-
niously in Venice, you can visit the **garden of the Querini Stampalia Foundation**,
near Campo Santa Maria Formosa, restored by *Carlo Scarpa* around 1962. ⌐ p. 107

What were the famous Serenissima war galleys called?

They were called *triremi* because the rowers, who used to row to the rhythm of a
drum played astern, were seated in rows of three. They were agile and fast, and
sank enemy ships with their rams and prow cannons.

What are the Tre Pili?

They are three great ship masts opposite the portal of the
Basilica di San Marco, from which the flags of Italy, Saint
Mark and the European Union wave on important days.

Which artists were so fascinated by Venice that they decided to move to the city or to immortalize it in their work?

A great many, in all ages and of all nationalities: among them,
famous painters like *Auguste Renoir*, *Claude Monet* and *William
Turner*, musicians like *Richard Wagner* and writers like *Francesco
Petrarca*, *Johann Wolfgang Goethe*, *Stendhal*, *Lord Byron*, *John
Ruskin*, *Friedrich Nietzsche*, *Henry James*, *Rainer Maria Rilke*,
Marcel Proust, *Thomas Mann* and *Gabriele D'Annunzio*.

What do Calle "del Pistor", "del Pestrin" and "del Fruttari-ol" mean, and why are there so many in Venice?

CALLE
DEL PISTOR

They are street names which occur often because they
were common trades: *pistor* is Venetian for baker,
pestrin for milkman and *fruttariol* means greengrocer.

Tradition

The gondola

The gondola has been the typical Venetian boat for more than one thousand years. It was mainly used for transporting people, connecting the various parts of the city, which used to have a lot more canals and less bridges. Today it is especially popular with the tourists visiting Venice.

The gondola is 11 metres long: it is painted black ∼ p. 79, with seven layers of a water-proofing paint, whose composition is secret. It has a long hull, a flat bottom to float on the lagoon's shallow waters and a slightly asymmetric shape: this enables the **gondolier** to correct its direction by rowing with just one oar. Each gondola is made up of about 280 wood pieces and belongs to its gondolier.

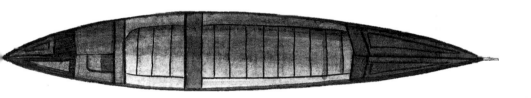

The palina

It is the coloured-stripe pole to which the gondola is tied, painted in the noble families' colours; it looks like a stick of candy rock.

How to row a gondola

The gondolier

He is the oarsman who rows "alla Veneta" (Venetian style), that is, standing and using just one oar. He wears a straw hat, black trousers and a striped shirt.

He knows all the canals of Venice, even the most hidden ones and, according to legend, he has webbed feet that enable him to walk on water. I wonder if it's true?

The "fero" (iron)

It is a six-toothed decorative piece symbolizing the six *sestieri* ⌒ p. 31 into which the city is divided: *Castello, San Marco, Cannaregio, Dorsoduro, San Polo, Santa Croce.* The seventh tooth on the other side represents the *Giudecca island.* ⌒ p. 113

The curved part above the teeth has the shape of the doge's hat, symbol of the power and protection exercised over the city.

The forcola

It's the *rowing lock* which supports the oar in eight different positions to give the gondola different directions. The forcola is carved from one single wooden block, usually walnut, pear or cherry.

The squero

It is the shipyard in which gondolas are repaired and built, an extremely ancient and complex craft. The oldest one is the **Squero di San Trovaso**, located between the Ponte dell'Accademia and the Zattere. Just three or four gondolas a year are built in each squero.

Special gondolas

The wedding gondola is decorated with flowers and the gondoliers are dressed in white instead of wearing the usual uniform. Funeral gondolas, which travel the distance to the cemetery p. 66, are decorated with gilded angels.

A gondola tour
To go on a gondola tour, all you have to do is contact any gondolier; you can see them practically everywhere. One of the many gondolier co-operatives is in Piazza San Marco in front of the columns; another one is at the Rialto Bridge, near the water bus landing. The tour usually lasts about 40-45 minutes; prices are fixed, but it is better to agree on them before.
A maximum of five or six people can travel in a gondola.
For information: the Gondola Service.
telephone 041 5285075

Boats

On these pages you can see some of the boats you'll find in Venice.

Regatta boats

They are the typical boats for competitions and they are called *Gondolino, Caorlina, Mascareta, Pupparin,* and *Disdotona.*

The Caorlina

As shown by its name, this six-oar boat comes from the city of *Caorle*; it was used to transport fruit and vegetables to the *Rialto market*; nowadays you will see it mainly in regattas.

The Pupparin

It is a colourful, slim and asymmetrical boat, which looks a lot like a gondola; its name comes from the fact that the aft oarsman rows standing on a sort of small platform.

The Disdotona

It takes its name from the number of oarsmen (eighteen). There is also the **Dodesona** (twelve) and the **Quatordesona** (fourteen). It opens the parade of boats during the *Historical Regatta* p. 63, and represents the different *rowing clubs*.

Fishing and leisure boats

These are the *Topo*, the *Sanpierota*, the *Bragozzo*, the *Sandolo* and the *S'ciopon*.

The Topo (or *Topa*)

It is one of the most common boats: it can have a sail if it is used for fishing, or an engine for carrying small loads.

The Bragozzo

It is a fishing boat used in the lagoon; typical of the area around Chioggia, the bragozzo can be recognized by the brightly coloured decorations painted all over its hull; it used to have a sail, but today it has an engine.

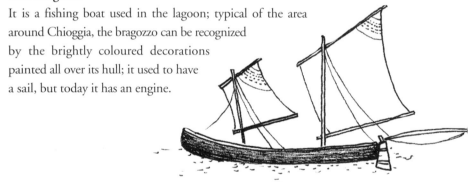

The S'ciopon

Its particularly flat keel makes it suitable for excursions in very shallow water.

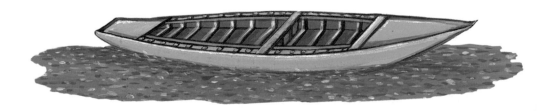

The boats of the ACTV (Venetian Transport Corporation)

The vaporetto (water bus)
It's slower than a motorboat and calls at all stops, but it is the best option for a relaxing sightseeing cruise (for example down the Grand Canal).

The motoscafo
A nimbler and faster water bus, it should be taken when in a hurry: it calls at fewer stops.

The motonave
A kind of giant vaporetto which connects Venice with the lagoon islands in high season. In summer Venetians use the motonave from Riva dei Schiavoni to go to the beach on the Lido .

The ACTV landing stage

It is a floating structure where you wait for the *vaporetto* or *motoscafo* to arrive; it has a sign indicating the name of the stop and it is sheltered.

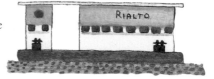

The bricola
It is made of rough wooden poles which are driven into the lagoon to mark water ways for boats.

Bitta

Other boats

Along the Venice canals, apart from the boats which carry all kinds of goods and the *vaporetti* (water buses), you can see *garbage-collection boats, taxis, fire-brigade, ambulance* and *police* motorboats.

Garbage collection boat

You can see them at dawn as they pick up the garbage put out the night before along the canals.

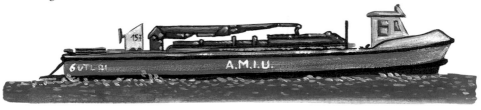

The taxi

You'll see it quite often dashing along the city canals. It allows you to cover water distances very quickly, but it generally has quite expensive fares.

Emergency boats

They are the only boats which can speed down the canals or even the Grand Canal in case of dire emergency. The fireboat is equipped with powerful hoses which use water pumped directly out of the canals to put out the fires.

Fire-boat

Police-boat

Ambulance

The Carnival

During the Serenissima Republic Carnival lasted practically six months, during which people celebrated from morning till evening. The Carnival started in October and continued until midnight on **Martedì Grasso** (shrove Tuesday), when a puppet representing the Carnival used to be burnt in Piazza San Marco and bells announced the beginning of *Lent*. During that period the city partied and everybody wore masks. Nobility and commoners, rich and poor alike hid behind their disguise and enjoyed mingling without being recognized. Piazza San Marco and the other *campi* and *campielli* p. 29-30 of the city became huge theatre stages on which all sorts of entertainment were organized: theatre shows, parties, concerts, balls, games, amusements and fireworks.

Carnival Games

During Carnival, the Serenissima government tolerated everything and every excess seemed to be allowed. The common people were offered numerous opportunities for entertainment and street attractions, like *human pyramids* or *stilt races*, organized by teams of skilled acrobats. A joyful, festive atmosphere reigned in the whole city, which was invaded by actors, musicians, mimes, skilled jugglers, fortune tellers and acrobats. Everywhere street vendors sold *frittole* and other typical Carnival sweet fare. p. 59

The Stocking Society

It was a merry brigade of young noble men who wore colourful stockings with an embroidered coat-of-arms. They organized some Carnival attractions, such as bull races. A "stocking society", the *Compagnia della Calza* o *dei Antichi* still exists today, and is very active in Carnival celebrations.

Carnival nowadays

The Carnival was abolished by Napoleon at the end of the 1700s, when it was at the height of its splendour. After a long period during which this festival was forgotten, the town authorities started organizing it again in 1979. Nowadays, just like in the old times, dances, parties, concerts and theatre shows are organized. Bizarre and fanciful costumes mix with traditional ⌒ p. 54 and 18th century ones. Fancy-dress characters coming from all over the world crowd Venetian squares, but especially Piazza San Marco and its cafés.

The make-up artists of Piazza San Marco

You haven't got a mask? Don't worry: in the Piazzetta dei Leoncini near the Basilica (but also under the arches of the Procuratie and Palazzo Ducale), you will find groups of skilful make-up artists who will paint a wonderful carnival mask with arabesques and sequins on your face for a small sum.

Costumes

Traditional Carnival costumes from 16th century comic theatre of **Commedia dell'Arte**.

Pantalone

He's an old, mean and grumpy Venetian merchant, whose servants are Brighella and Arlecchino. His role is that of keeping in check young people's plans and servants' trickery. He's got a white beard and hair and wears a woollen beret, red stockings, pantaloons, a black cape and slippers.

Arlecchino

He is without doubt the most famous character. His suit is made of colourful patches, old leftovers of different cloths gathered here and there. He's always hungry, and a lazy glutton. He tries to take the world as it come, gaining maximum benefit from it, cunningly deceiving others, but he's often the victim of Brighella's tricks. He's a top acrobat, and very good at making all kinds of somersaults and pirouettes.

Brighella

He's Arlecchino's side-kick, a quick servant and a busybody. He wears a long white costume with a green hem and he's got a long curled-up moustache. He's as cunning as a fox and has no scruples in stealing money from his master. He can sing and play the guitar.

Balanzone

Bolognese doctor and gourmet, he is dressed in black from head to toes like scientists, professors and lawyers of his time. He's got a big fat stomach, round spectacles and wears a beret. He sometimes uses Latin words to impress the people he's talking to.

Pulcinella

A jester and lazybones, he loves joking and playing the clown. He's all dressed in white except the mask, which is black with a long beak-like nose. He wears a white cone hat.

Colombina

She's a vain and mischievous young maid, dressed in 18th century fashion. Easy and a bit of a flirt, she's got Arlecchino wrapped around her finger.

The Black Death doctor

To avoid contagion during outbreaks of the Black Death, the doctor used to wear a strange uniform: a hooked-nose mask which looked like a bird's beak, and which was filled with medicinal herbs and essences to disinfect the air.

Music and theatre

Here are two great artists who left a mark not only in the Venice of their times, but in the history of theatre and music: *Antonio Vivaldi* and *Carlo Goldoni*.

Antonio Vivaldi (1678-1741)

The son of a San Marco violinist, he was ordained a priest after receiving an excellent musical education. He was called *the Red Priest* because of his hair colour, and he composed many operas as well as pieces of sacred and profane music. His works were sung by the *Orphaned Girls Choir* of the church of the *Pietà*. This church, where Vivaldi was violin and choir master, became famous thanks to the great composer's works.

He wrote 447 concertos for string and wind instruments; his most famous work, *The Four Seasons*, became enormously successful all over Europe. Many concertos by the Venetian composer are still performed today in the **church of the Pietà**.

Chiesa della Pietà.
Riva degli Schiavoni
For information and tickets:
Telephone 041 5231096.
Open every day
9 a.m. - 2 p.m.

Music
Venice today offers quite a varied musical panorama;
Pitura Freska (Fresh Paint: 'pitura' also means money
in Venetian dialect) are a reggae band who sing in Venetian
dialect and have become very popular.

Carlo Goldoni (1707-1793)

The great Venetian playwright wrote more than 250 plays, based especially on the characters of the *Commedia dell'Arte*: *Pantalone, Arlecchino, Brighella, Balanzone, Colombina* and many others. ⌒ p. 54

In his plays, Goldoni accurately described life in 18th century Venice, making fun of the laziness of the aristocracy and satirizing the customs of that period.

He did not like the way the characters of the Commedia dell'Arte improvised without a script, and re-introduced the written text, giving great emphasis to popular characters and a realistic tone.

Among his most successful works: *Arlecchino Servant of Two Masters* (1745), *The Mistress of the Inn* (1753), *The Rusteghi* (1760), *The Chioggia Fights* (1762) and *One of the last evenings of the Carnival* (1762), the last play he wrote in Italy before leaving for the court of the King of France, where he remained until his death.

Casa di Goldoni Museum
It is possible to visit the house where the writer was born, which has today become a museum and a centre for theatrical studies.
San Polo 2794
Telephone 041 5236353
Temporarily closed for restoration

Comic Art
A lot of the Disney artists who draw for the Italian edition of Mickey Mouse Magazine are of Venetian origin, like Romano Scarpa. Corto Maltese undoubtedly deserves a place of honour. He's a Venetian sailor created by the late Hugo Pratt, and is always involved in some dangerous adventure or on a journey to exotic destinations.

Yummy treats

Venetian cuisine offers a wealth of appetizing and delicious recipes, such as the famous **risotto** called "all'onda" for its creamy appearance, the **carpaccio** (thin slices of raw meat seasoned with oil, lemon and scales of parmesan cheese), **Venetian-style liver** (cooked with onions), **polenta** and **seafood dishes** galore.

If you also have a sweet tooth you'll be able to taste real delicacies, which the Venetians call "golosessi"; in addition to the famous **tiramisù** (which is also well-known abroad) there is a rich assortment of various sweet foods. In bakeries you can still find **cakes** and **biscuits** prepared according to ancient tradition. Here are some of them.

Bussolai

They have a ring shape and can be savoury or sweet, in which case they can also have an "s" shape and are called *buranei*, because they are typical products of the Burano island. ⌒ p. 120

Other traditional biscuits are the thin **baicoli, basi de dama** (lady's kisses), made with chocolate-filled almond paste, and **lingue de suocera** (mother-in-law's tongues!), with chocolate icing.

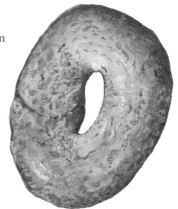

Spumiglie

These are meringues made with sugar and whipped egg whites and look like sea froth. Other traditional Venetian products are **sbreghette**, crunchy biscuits made with almonds and fennel seeds, and **pignoletti** (or *pignoccae*), soft cakes made with almonds and pine seeds.

Fritole

They are a kind of sweet fritter eaten at Carnival; the dough is mixed with pine seeds and raisins. There are three different kinds of fritola: filled with *crema pasticcera*, a kind of custard, with *zabaione* (egg and liqueur cream) or with no filling, which are called "alla Veneziana" (Venetian style).

Crostoli or galani

They are traditional Carnival sweets, made with thin fried dough powdered with icing sugar. In other parts of Italy they have different names: *nastri* or *chiacchere*.

Zaleti

The name of these typical Venetian biscuits comes from the yellow corn flour with which they are made. Would you like to make them to surprise your friends? It's not at all difficult: just go to the next page.

Recipe: how to bake zaleti

Ingredients: 300g corn flour, 300g white flour, 3 eggs, 150g caster sugar, 2 litres milk, 100g beer yeast, 100g raisins, 60g pine seeds, the grated rind of a lemon, 150g butter, a pinch of salt and one of vanilla, icing sugar.

1. Beat the eggs with the sugar, then add the white flour and the corn flour.

2. Moisten and wring the raisins. Put the butter in a bowl, which you then stand over a pan of simmering water until the butter melts.

3. Mix the beer yeast with the milk and add it to the dough together with the raisins, the pine seeds, the lemon rind, the butter, a pinch of salt and one of vanilla.

4. Mix until you get a soft dough which you then cut and shape into little ovals. Put them onto a buttered oven tray and bake them in the oven at 160°C for 25-30 minutes.
Dust them over with the icing sugar.

Let's play together

Tartaglia and Arlecchina in fancy dress

Colour them in and they will be ready for the Carnival with their beautiful costumes.

Important festivals and events

Carnival

It is celebrated two weeks before Lent. Venetians and especially tourists dress up in fancy costumes and masks. A number of different events and shows are organized every year. ↷ p. 53

Feast of St. Mark

On the 25th of April, St. Mark's day, the custom is for every Venetian to present his sweetheart with a **bocolo** (a red rose bud). The traditional dish for this festival is **risi e bisi**, a risotto with peas.

Festival of Redentore

On the third weekend of July a **bridge of boats** is built to connect the *Zattere* with the *church of Redentore* on the *Giudecca island.* ↷ p. 114 All Venetians dine and drink on boats in the *Giudecca canal.* The festival ends with spectacular **fireworks**.

Vogalonga

It is held on the first Sunday after *Ascension Day* and mainly Venetian rowing schools take part, even though participation is open. People row for 32 kilometres – from *Bacino di San Marco* to *Burano* and back – starting at 9 a.m. and finishing around 3 p.m.

Historical Regatta

On the first Sunday of September there is a parade of historic craft on the *Grand Canal*, with oarsmen wearing historical costumes. ⌐ p. 47

St. Martin

On the 11th of November *Saint Martin*, who cut his cape in half to give it to a poor beggar, is remembered. Venetian children roam the streets singing the **song of San Martino**, to the sound of beaten pots and lids. ⌐ p. 138 People eat a **cake** decorated with sugared almonds and chocolates in the shape of the sword-bearing saint on horseback.

Feast of "La Salute"

To celebrate the end of the Black Death ⌐ p. 79, Venetians who survived the 1630 outbreak commissioned the architect *Baldassarre Longhena* with the design of the great *Chiesa di Santa Maria della Salute* (*salute* means health in Italian). The religious festival was established at the end of the 17th century as a token of devotion to the Virgin Mary who had freed the city from the plague; celebrated on the 21st of November, it is still very much felt by the Venetians. For the occasion a **bridge of boats** is built across the Grand Canal, connecting *Santa Maria del Giglio* to the church of "La Salute".

Su e zo per i ponti

A marathon which takes place on the second Sunday in March up and down the city bridges, attracting participants of all ages, from all walks of life and from all over the world.

Traditional products

Masks

In many stores and craft workshops, you can find all the traditional *Commedia dell'Arte* masks from *Pantalone* to *Arlecchino* ⌒ p. 54-55, 57, as well as many others of all shapes and colours, made by hand out of leather or papier maché.

Carnival hats

With or without bells, in the strangest and fanciest shapes, these bizarre, colourful, velvet hats have been on sale practically everywhere for a few years now.

Miniature gondolas

In plastic, wood or glass they are one of the most renowned symbols of Venice.

Marble paper

Many craftsmen produce it with a complex process, through which beautiful shades and patterns of different colours are obtained. ⌒ p. 157

Gondolier's T-shirt and hat

On the stalls at Rialto or on Piazza San Marco, you'll be able to buy the classical gondolier's uniform: striped T-shirt and straw hat with red or blue ribbon.

Venetian slippers

The classical gondolier's slippers are in velvet and, to avoid slipping, the sole is lined with bicycle-tyre rubber. They can be used not only at home but also outdoors, and are available in an infinite variety of shades: you can find them on the Rialto bridge too.

Murano glass objects

You can find animal families and a remarkable production of miniature objects, made with the traditional Murano *glass lamp-working* technique.
↷ p. 117

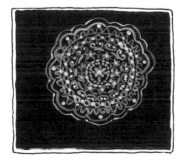

Lace

Lace is a typical product especially from the *island of Burano* , where women still embroider with the *Venezia stitch.* ↷ p. 120

 # Oddities

What are "murazzi"?

That's the name of the *break-waters* that protect the beaches of *Lido* p. 115 and *Pellestrina* from the erosion of the sea.

Where were the first "coffee shops" in Europe opened?

In Venice, in Piazza San Marco; of the tens of coffee shops which opened in the piazza between the end of the 1600s and the beginning of the 1700s, only **Caffè Florian** has survived until the present day. Inaugurated in 1720, it was once called *Alla Venezia trionfante* (the triumphant Venice); it then took the name of its owner, *Floriano Francesconi*.

Which is the only Piazza in Venice?

Piazza San Marco. p. 81 The other piazzas, big and small, are called *campi* and *campielli.* p. 29-31

What does the Venetian word "caigo" mean?

It's the fog that often envelopes the city, especially in autumn and winter, giving it a special, mysterious atmosphere.

Which important English poet swam up the Grand Canal?

Lord Byron, during his stay in Venice in 1818.

Where is the Venice cemetery?

On the *island of San Michele*, near Murano: important artists are buried there, like the composer *Igor Stravinskij* and the poet *Ezra Pound*.

Who was the "spezier"?

He was the pharmacist from whom people also bought spices and preserves, as well as coffee and *Indian salt*, that is sugar.

Who were the "acquaroli"?

They were a syndicate of boatmen who used to row all the way from the lagoon to a branch of the river Brenta to bring back water which, despite the reservoirs, was never enough.

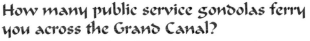

How many public service gondolas ferry you across the Grand Canal?

There are seven *traghetti*, located at *San Marcuola, Santa Sofia, San Silvestro, San Tomà, San Samuele, S. M. del Giglio* and *Punta della Dogana*. The crossing costs just under £ 1000. p. 156

What are the "pàtere"?

They are small stone decorations on house walls; often round, they picture real or fantastic animals.

Which is the only bridge in Venice that still has no railings?

It's the bridge on the *rio di San Felice* in Cannaregio, behind *Strada Nuova*. Once no Venetian bridges had railings, so it was very easy to fall in the water!

What were the "fondaci" for?

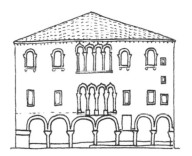

They were the rich merchants' homes and warehouses. Their main feature was a portico on the ground floor (such as the *fondaco dei Turchi*, or the *fondaco dei Tedeschi*, which you can see on the Grand Canal). They had a double function: they were a dwelling, but also a warehouse for the goods and a place where business was done.

Nature

Fish of the lagoon
Small animals to look for
The cats of Venice
Acqua alta
What to wear

Fish of the lagoon

How many different fish are there in the lagoon?
If you go to the **Rialto market**, you will see all kinds of fish being sold. Do you know any of their names? Let's have a look together.

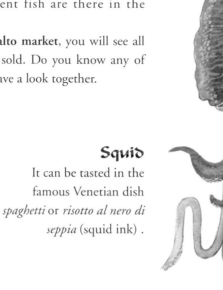

Squid
It can be tasted in the famous Venetian dish *spaghetti* or *risotto al nero di seppia* (squid ink) .

Mantis shrimp
It's a crustacean, which the Venetians call *canocia*.

Branzino
This voracious predator is big and tasty, one of the most appreciated fish in Venetian cuisine.

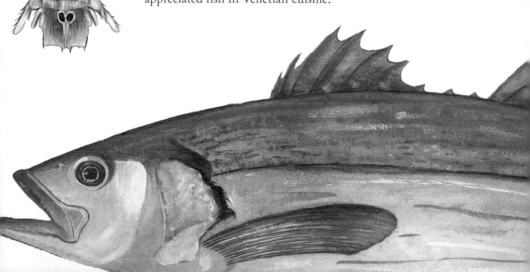

Schia

A tiny lagoon shrimp,
eaten with yellow *polenta*.

Sole

A flat-bodied fish which
hides on the sandy
sea bottom.

Crab

When it sheds its shell
it's called "moeca" and
it can be eaten fried.

Vieri

They are wicker baskets placed in
special spots of the lagoon or carried
on boat sides, to keep crabs, eels and
other fish alive.

Eel

It is called *bisato* in Venetian, and it's a very long fish that looks a bit like a snake.

Mussels

The Venetians call them *peoci* and they are delicious with spaghetti or *tagliolini* (thin noodles).

The mussel-breeding rows

There are mussel farms in the lagoon. The mussels stick to the threads of the rows.

Triglia

It's a mullet with a distinctive reddish colour and is delicious fried.

Let's play together

A lucky catch

Bepi the fisherman is fishing. Can you tell which fishing rod has caught the little fish?

Small animals to look for

The animals you'll see on these pages are rather common: you'll see them while strolling in Venice.

Sparrows

They are always looking for food, and together with the pigeon they are the most common birds.

Pigeons

Venetians call them *colombi*, they are the undisputed kings of Piazza San Marco.

Seagulls

Called *cocài*, you can see them flying low over the lagoon looking for fish.

72

Swallows

In the hot season you can hear them
twitter and whistle above the roofs.

Mice

There are common sewer mice
and *pantegane* (water rats).

Cats

There are lots and lots
everywhere: on doorsteps, on
windowsills, in shop windows,
on well curbs, even on boats!
If you like cats, go to the next
page and you'll find lots
more information.

The cats of Venice

The lion is the symbol of Venice, but the real lord of *calli* and *campielli* is another feline greatly loved by the Venetians: its cousin, the cat.

While strolling about you'll see lots of them, lazily curled up in the sun or busy chasing pigeons. Sometimes you'll even see them quietly resting among the goods in a shop window. In every sestiere, old ladies feed them with leftovers.
Rialto market stall keepers often give them something to eat, while the children playing in the campi keep them company.

The cat island
The island of San Clemente, where the asylum once was, has today become "cats' island": since 1990 it is, in fact, inhabited by moggies cared for by Dingo.

There are whole colonies of cats fed and looked after by Dingo, an association which supplies food, medical care and small shelters for cold winter nights.
You can see these little houses lined with old blankets in some areas of Venice: cats seek shelter there in winter to keep warm.

The cats' bookshop
Libreria San Pantalon
Dorsoduro 3950
Closed on Sundays
10a.m. - 7.30p.m.

The San Pantalon bookshop is near the university
of Ca' Foscari and, apart from stocking lots of
children's books, it specializes in cats. You'll find
everything regarding cats there, games and all sorts
of books. In the shop window you will see Rosa, the
two owners' red cat, curled up on a pile of books.

Let's play together
The lost kitten
Mitten the kitten has got lost in the maze of Venetian calli.
Can you help him find the way home?

Acqua alta

It happens every year between October and April. The area of San Marco is the first to go under water because it's the city's lowest point. The 1966 floods, which caused disasters in the whole of Italy, brought about an exceptionally high water level which reached nearly 2 m in height above the average sea level, causing very severe damage to the city.

Why Piazza San Marco gets flooded

Rain water is drained from Piazza San Marco through gutters which flow into the Grand Canal. Because of the principle of communicating vessels, following exceptional tides the water from the Grand Canal enters the drain gutters flooding the piazza.

What causes flood tides

They are caused by:
1) high tide brought about by attraction the of the moon (*astronomical tide*);
2) variations in atmospheric pressure which cause strong winds, such as the *Scirocco* and the *Bora*, which push water into the lagoon from the Adriatic Sea.
3) progressive sinking of the soil (30 centimetres in this century).

Boardwalks

When a high tide is expected, Venetians arrange wooden boardwalks for pedestrians in the city's busiest spots, such as the areas around Rialto and Piazza San Marco.

What people used to do

Back in the times of the Serenissima Republic ↷ p. 20, the dirt accumulating in the canals was dredged regularly to prevent the mud level from rising too much.
Good navigability of the canals was fundamental for a city whose power and wealth was founded on sea trade.

Solutions to protect Venice from acqua alta

1) in the canals, cleaning and maintaining the *rii* ↷ p. 29 to eliminate the mud accumulating on the bottom;
2) on the Lido and Pellestrina islands, widening of beaches and strengthening of dykes;
3) reconstruction of jetties at harbour entrances and of sandbanks, that is, the emerging land which limits the wave motion;
4) **Móse**: it's a project under preliminary discussion which provides for the installation of an electro-mechanical system of protective barriers to adjust the ebb and flow of tides at the harbour entrances of Lido, Malamocco and Chioggia.

Insula Project

It is carried out by the Town Council for the maintenance of the city – especially those parts of Venice hidden by canals - and provides for a series of repairs which will have to continue in cycles. In addition to dredging up the canals, where the mud tends to set in layers, *Insula* operates to consolidate the foundations of buildings, which are damaged by the water motion caused by motor-boats, and to restore the pavement of *calli* and *campi*. ↷ p. 29

What to wear

If it's sunny

Comfortable walking shoes (remember that in Venice you'll go practically everywhere on foot, whether you like it or not!), shorts, T-shirt or vest if it's very hot, or pullover and long trousers if it's still cold; a hat if it's very sunny; in your rucksack you should put a bottle of water, a snack, pen case, camera (if you've got one) and your guidebook.

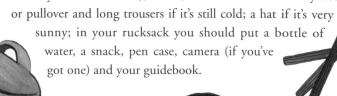

If it rains or the water level is high

Rubber-soled shoes or wellies, (roll up your trousers in case of *acqua alta*) and a warm pullover if it's cold; you should also put a light rain jacket in your rucksack.

 **Oddities**

What's the "felze"?

A small closed cabin which sheltered gondola passengers from the cold and ensured a certain amount of privacy. ➔ p. 43

Have gondolas always been painted black?

No, they once were richly decorated and painted, but a 1633 decree of the Serenissima Republic ordered they should all be painted black to stop luxury competitions and vain showing off among the nobility.

How many people died during the 1576 and 1630 plagues?

During the two outbreaks, the Black Death halved the population of Venice: 100,000 people died, among them *Titian, the great Venetian painter*. The end of the 1630 outbreak was celebrated by building the *Church of Santa Maria della Salute* and establishing the **procession** on the **boat bridge** for the *festival of "La Salute"*. *Salute* means health in Italian. ➔ p. 63

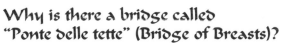

What are the Bauta, Tricorno and Tabarro?

In order not to be recognized while walking around Venice, the nobility used to wear the *bauta* (a white mask which covered nearly the whole face), together with a black silk hood and a lace cape. They also wore the *tricorno* (a black three-pointed hat) and the *tabarro* (a large black cloak).

Why is there a bridge called "Ponte delle tette" (Bridge of Breasts)?

It's near Rialto ➔ p. 92, in the area which used to be reserved for courtesans; according to legend, they attracted clients by showing their assets from windows.

If it's sunny

Piazza San Marco
The Palazzo Ducale
The Ponte di Rialto
The Ghetto
The church of Santa Maria Gloriosa dei Frari
The Scuola Grande di San Rocco
The campo of Santi Giovanni e Paolo
The church of miracles
The church of San Pietro di Castello
The Arsenale and the museum of Naval History

Piazza San Marco

The Piazza

It has been defined as the most beautiful living room in the whole world, and it has always been the heart of life in Venice. It is surrounded by the **Procuratie Nuove** and **Vecchie**, by the **Basilica di San Marco** and by the **Torre dell'Orologio**.

Chiesa di San Geminiano

The **Napoleonic Wing** was added under Napoleon's rule, who wanted reception rooms and ballrooms. Today it is the seat of the **Correr museum.** ↻ p. 106 The new building took the place of the *church of San Geminiano* , which used to face the *Basilica di San Marco* on the opposite side of the Piazza.

The Basilica

The Basilica di San Marco was originally the Doge's private chapel and State ceremonies took place there. After being destroyed and rebuilt twice, it finally took the present shape, with a *greek-cross* plan (with four equal arms) and five domes. Even though it has been added to through the centuries with elements and decorations which show a great mixture of different styles, the church remains essentially Byzantine. The deep influence of the East (which has always traded and had exchanges with Venice) is revealed especially in the use of *golden-background decorations* and in the *mosaic technique*, which make the Basilica look like a palace out of the "Arabian Nights".

Basilica di San Marco
telephone 041 5225205
open every day
9.30 a.m. - 5.00 p.m.
2.00 p.m. - 5.00 p.m. Sunday and holidays

A detail of the Basilica's floors

The Basilica's mosaics

The church is entirely decorated with wonderful mosaics, which, with floors, walls and domes, cover a total surface of over 4,000 square metres. Outside, you will see the façade's mosaics (like the one that pictures the *Theft of St. Mark's remains from Alexandria in Egypt* ↷ p. 17); inside, you will walk over a wonderful oriental rug made of tiny colourful marble and porphyry tiles, which create intricate geometric patterns. You will see other glittering mosaics in the **Pentecost dome** (the *Holy Ghost descending upon Apostles*), in the **Baptistery** (the *cycle of St. John the Baptist's life*) and in the small **Creation dome** (24 mosaics depicting the *Genesis*).

In the huge **Ascension dome** there is the glittering image of *Christ in glory, with the Virgin Mary, two angels and the 12 Apostles*. Have a look also at the other wonders kept in the Basilica: the rich **Treasury of San Marco,** which consists of magnificent Italian and Byzantine works of art, and the **Pala d'Oro**, a glittering icon of enamel and precious gems made in the 10th century.

Campanile di San Marco
telephone 041 5224064
9.30 a.m. – 5.00 p.m. (winter)
9.30 a.m. – 7.30 p.m. (spring)
9.30 a.m. – 9.30 p.m. (summer)

Venice from up high: on the Campanile

When you get to the top of the *bell tower of San Marco* (there's a lift), on fine days you will enjoy a wonderful sight: all around you the wonderful spectacle of Venice seen from its rooftops!
The *campanile* is affectionately called by Venetians *el paron de casa* (the master of the house). It has five bells which the Venetians have names for: *Marangona, Trottiera, Nona, Pregadì* and *Renghiera.*
You'll hear them when the hour strikes.

In 1902 the ancient campanile collapsed, luckily with no casualties; it was later rebuilt exactly as the original; the reconstruction took a decade.

From the top of the campanile, in 1609 Galileo Galilei gave Doge Leonardo Donà a demonstration of how the telescope worked.

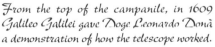

The Horses

Cast in almost pure bronze and then gilded,
the horses of the Basilica di San Marco are the symbol of Venetian freedom.
In 1797, when Venice was occupied by the French, they were taken to Paris by
Napoleon as war loot, but in 1815, with the fall of the French emperor, they were
brought back to Venice. The original horses are kept inside the Basilica, while the
ones outside are replicas.

The Tetrarchs

On the side of the Basilica facing the *Piazzetta*, near the two columns, you will see four figures called the *Tetrarchs*. They were taken as war loot from the East, like the majority of the church's decorations. A legend says they are four foreigners turned to stone for having attempted to steal some treasure. In reality, they apparently picture the emperor *Diocletian* and the other members of the Roman Empire tetrarchy.

The Torre dell'Orologio

The huge blue-enamelled clock-face, dotted with golden stars and planets, is a real **calendar**: it shows the time, the months, moon phases and the **zodiac** as well.
It therefore provided very important information to the Venetian galleys that sailed Eastbound from the *Bacino di San Marco*. This clock, built in the 15th century, was a wonder of its time

According to legend, once the work was over, the makers of the clock and the statues of the *Mori* were blinded so they could never again build anything like this anywhere in the world.

If you happen to be in Venice during *Ascension week*, at the striking of the hour you'll be surprised to see the Three Wise Men come out of the side doors and bow to the Virgin and Child, who are placed in a niche above the clock.

The Moors

The two bronze statues of the *Mori* are like two huge robots with a complex mechanism, which strike every hour on a huge bell on top of the *Torre dell'Orologio*.

Let's play together

The Mosaics of the Basilica di San Marco

With your crayons, colour in these mosaics
from the Basilica di San Marco. Then, as in a
treasure hunt, when you visit the Basilica you
can look for the originals inside.

The Palazzo Ducale

The *Palazzo Ducale* was built in the 9th century. Originally a fortified castle, it was successively destroyed by many fires and later rebuilt in the 14th and 15th century as a grand example of Venetian gothic style. ⌐ p. 36 If you look at the **loggia arches**, you'll see the refined battlement in *Istria stone*, carved to make it look like lace. On the outside the palace has three interesting **sculptures** decorating the corners: *The judgement of Solomon, Adam and Eve with the Snake* and, near the *ponte della Paglia, The drunkenness of Noah*. Once through the main entrance, called **Porta della Carta**, you'll be in the **inner courtyard**. The Doge used to be crowned here, on top of the **Scala dei Giganti** (the stairway presided by the giants *Mars* and *Neptune*, symbols of the Republic's domain over earth and sea). The Palace was the Doge's residence, but also the seat of government and the magistrature. It had military comand, tribunals, prisons and the **Sala del Maggior Consiglio**, a huge hall where there are the **portraits of the first 76 Doges** and a painting by *Tintoretto*: **Paradise**, one of the largest paintings in the world (24.65 x 7.45 m). In addition to the Tintoretto, in the palace you will find other paintings by famous artists of the Venetian Renaissance ⌐ p. 103 such as *Titian, Veronese* and *Palma il Giovane*. And don't miss the fantastic **Armoury**!

Palazzo Ducale
Telephone 041 2715911
open every day
9.00 a.m. - 7.00 p.m. from April to October (the ticket office closes at 5.30 p.m.)
9.00 a.m. - 5.00 p.m. from November to March (the ticket office closes at 3.30 p.m.)

During the visit, you will get an idea of what Venice must have been like at the time of its greatest splendour, when it traded with the East and was called the *Repubblica Serenissima.*  p. 20 In those years, the bodies of the executed were often displayed under the external colonnade of the Palazzo Ducale, to show people what would happen if State laws were broken. Common criminals were jailed in the **Prigioni** but, if considered dangerous, they ended up in the *pozzi*, dark and wet dungeons on the ground floor which were often flooded in case of *acqua alta* ⌒ p. 76 (which also solved the problem of overpopulation in the prisons!).

At the times of the Serenissima, it was no joke if one didn't behave properly!

The lion's mouths
They were used to collect anonymous complaints about citizens, which were slipped into the "Bocche di leone". One is in the Loggia of the Palazzo Ducale, the other one is in the Sala della Bussola.

The Secret Itineraries
It is definitely worthwhile to follow the *Secret Itineraries*, a tour inside the Palace which lasts about 90 minutes, for small groups of twenty people. You will discover the **Piombi** prisons (Giacomo Casanova was the only man to ever escape from here), the **Camera del tormento** (the Torture chamber where the prisoners, hung by their wrists, were questioned), the **sala dei Tre Capi** of the *Consiglio dei Dieci* and the **stanza dell'Inquisizione** (State Inquisitors' Room), as well as the hidden passages and maze-like corridors of the palace.

Secret Itineraries
telephone 041 5209070
open every day
leaving at 10.00 a.m.
and 11.30 a.m.
Book in advance

Giacomo Casanova

In 1755 *Casanova*, the great Venetian adventurer and libertine, was imprisoned in the "Piombi", wooden cells situated under the lead (piombo in Italian) roof of the Palazzo Ducale. He nevertheless managed to escape by making a hole in the ceiling, thanks to the help of another prisoner, *Father Balbi*. Casanova himself described his extraordinary escape in the book "*My escape from the Piombi*". His gaoler, who had failed in the task of watching the prisoner, was himself condemned to prison by the Serenissima government.

The Ponte dei Sospiri

It is called like this (The *Bridge of Sighs*) because the prisoners crossing it on their way from the palace tribunals to the prisons or to execution, threw a last glance at the Venetian lagoon and sighed in nostalgia for their lost freedom.

The Doge

The doge, from the Latin word *dux* (commander), was the governor of Venice and the Head of the Republic. Elected for life by the *Maggior Consiglio* (the council which convened members of the Venetian noble families, registered in the *Libro d'Oro* ↷ p. 21), he was the symbol of the *Serenissima*. His power was more representative than real, though, since he could not make any decision without the approval of his *Six Councillors* (who represented the six *sestieri* of Venice ↷ p. 31), and he was subject to the control of the *Consiglio dei Dieci*. He wore the *corno*, the doge's round-tipped beret, decorated with gems and precious fabrics, such as velvet and damask. The doge's wife was called *dogaressa*.

Famous Venetian Doges

Among the 120 Doges who governed the Republic for 1100 years (from 697 to 1797), the first one was *Paoluccio Anafesto* and the last one *Ludovico Manin*, who abdicated – ending the Serenissima – when Napoleon invaded Venice. An important doge in the history of the Republic was *Enrico Dandolo* who, despite being blind and, by then, 90 years old, led the Crusaders to attack Constantinople: the victory brought huge commercial and economic advantages to Venice. It is said, instead, that *Andrea Gritti*, another famous doge who started his glorious career as general, died for a fatal sin of gluttony: a terrible eel indigestion!

A different fate befell the *Doge Giovanni Mocenigo* who denounced the philosopher *Giordano Bruno* to the inquisitors of the *Sant'Uffizio*, thus condemning him to the stake. According to an old legend, he was haunted for years by the philosopher's ghost, who apparently is still haunting the *Ca' Mocenigo Vecchia* now! There was only one doge who betrayed the Republic. His name was *Marino Falier* and in 1355 he was discovered at the head of a conspiracy. His thirst for power cost him dear, since he was immediately beheaded. His portrait in the *Sala del Maggior Consiglio*, unlike those of the other Doges, has been painted over with a black veil bearing a Latin inscription.

The two Columns

They are in *Piazza San Marco* overlooking the *Bacino*, and were brought from the East; they once marked the official entrance to Venice, since it could only be reached by sea. The Greek warrior *St. Theodore* (*Tòdaro* in Venetian), Venice's first patron saint, stands on top of one pillar, with his foot resting on the defeated dragon.
The other pillar bears the *winged lion*, emblem of *St. Mark*, who became the city's new patron saint. ⌒ p. 17

Bar Tòdaro
At the end of such an intense day, treat yourself to a special ice-cream from the bar near the two pillars. You can enjoy it while admiring the island of San Giorgio ⌒ p. 114

The space between the two pillars was the only place in Venice where gambling was allowed; it was also the scaffold where criminals were publicly executed. Hence the citizens' habit of avoiding it: popular superstition says it brings bad luck!

Let's play together

The pigeon of Piazza San Marco
What's Nino the pigeon flying over?
Join the dots to find out.

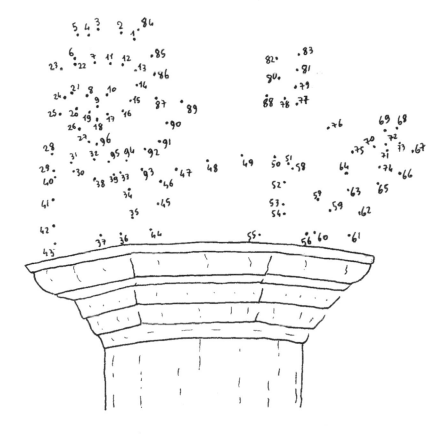

The Ponte di Rialto

It is one of the three bridges over the Grand Canal, with the *Ponte degli Scalzi* and the *Ponte dell'Accademia*.  p. 34 It surely is the most famous Venetian bridge and until the 1800's it was the only bridge connecting the two parts of the city divided by the Grand Canal. It used to be made of wood and it originally opened up to let through galleys, merchant ships and the Venetian fleet's great vessels. At the end of the 1500's it was rebuilt in stone at a cost of 250,000 ducats by *Antonio Da Ponte*, who won the competition beating famous Renaissance architects such as *Andrea Palladio* and *Jacopo Sansovino*. There are still a lot of **shops** on the steps of the Rialto bridge today, just like in the old times. From the balustrades you can enjoy wonderful views over the Grand Canal.

At the foot of the bridge there is the **Rialto open market**: the *erbarìa* (fruit, flowers and vegetables) and the *pescarìa* (fish, seafood and crustaceans), where fresh produce brought in every day by large barges is sold.

Osteria Al Pòrtego
This typical Venetian bàcaro, where you can taste appetizing cicheti ⌐ p. 25, is at the foot of the Rialto bridge, between Campo San Lio and the corte del Milion (where Marco Polo lived).

Osteria Alle Testiere
This small inn is in a side-street of Calle Lunga San Lio: few tables, but an exceptional chef who every day makes delicious recipes of the local traditional cuisine, mainly seafood. The inn takes its name Alle Testiere from two old headboards hung on the wall which, oddly enough, have been turned into shelves for glasses and bottles.

Spaghetteria-Snack Bar Tiziano
A cozy and pleasant place, not far from the Rialto Bridge, to have a quick snack or a pasta dish. If you are in a hurry, there is a wide selection of filled rolls, pizzas, "piadine", and sandwiches. If you have time to sit down, you can try one of the many dishes on the menu all of them reasonably priced.

The Ghetto

Apparently the word *ghetto* comes from the Venetian *getar*, which means to melt. In this area, in fact, there used to be a foundry, which the Venetians called *geto* (pouring), where around 1390 cannons were cast before it was moved to the Arsenale. ⌐ p. 99 With time the word ghetto was used to describe the place where Jews were gathered, confined on the island of *Gheto Novo*. In 1516 a decree of the *Council of Ten* in fact confined many Jews expelled from Spain in this particular area of Venice.

The word ghetto indicates still today the place where people of the same race, religion and nationality live. Jews in Venice had to live by very strict rules: at the curfew the gates guarded by Christian soldiers, who had to be paid by the Jewish community, were closed.

At night Jews were separated from the rest of the population. During the day they could leave the island, but had to wear identification berets and badges. They could lend money and work only as rag traders and in the medical profession.

Even though the Jewish district was enlarged, to include the *Gheto Vecio* and the *Gheto Novissimo*, the number of its inhabitants was always very high. In the 17th century more than 5000 Jews lived in the *Ghetto*. This explains the height - very unusual for Venice - of the Jewish district's houses, which can have seven or eight floors. With Napoleon's arrival in 1797 and later, when the Italian Kingdom was proclaimed (1866), the *Venetian Jewish Community* was granted freedom.

Hebrew Art museum
Campo del Ghetto Novo
telephone 041 715359
closed on Saturdays and Jewish Holidays
10.00 a.m. - 7.00 p.m. (summer)
10.00 a.m. - 5.30 p.m. (winter)
guided tours of the five synagogues leave
hourly starting at 10.30 a.m.

The church of Santa Maria Gloriosa dei Frari

The dimensions and height of the belfry of this great gothic church come second only to San Marco. Completed at the beginning of the 15th century, it was built by the Franciscan friars on the foundations of an earlier church. You will immediately spot a huge marble pyramid which will make you curious: it has an open door, which symbolizes the Otherworld, towards which the figures in a funereal procession are walking.

It is the **monument to Antonio Canova**, made in 1822 by the disciples of the great neo-classical sculptor. He had initially designed it for the painter **Titian's mausoleum**, which was never made due to lack of funds.

Chiesa dei Frari

The church also has several **Doge's tombs** (such as *Nicolò Tron*, *Giovanni Pesaro* and *Francesco Foscari*) and many art masterpieces: apart from the only statue by the sculptor *Donatello* kept in Venice (St. *John the Baptist*), you will see two important paintings by *Titian* (*Madonna di Ca' Pesaro* and, above the greater altar, the *Assumption of the Virgin Mary*) and one by *Giovanni Bellini* (the *Madonna enthroned with Child and Saints*). At the centre there is the **Friars' Choir**, a carved wood work by *Marco Cozzi*.

The Scuola Grande di San Rocco

St. Rocco, patron Saint of the plague-stricken, is the saint protecting this *Scuola Grande* ⌐ p. 27 spared by *Napoleon*, who, after invading Venice, with an 1806 decree closed down most *Scuole* and convents of the city. Once the Scuola was devoted to caring for the plague victims; today San Rocco is especially famous for its **paintings**, about 50 masterpieces made between 1564 and 1587 by *Jacopo Robusti* called *Il Tintoretto* (the nickname was because his father was a dyer). Apparently at first there had to be a competition to decide who was going to do the Scuola's decorations, in which many Veneto painters wanted to participate with their sketches, but Tintoretto was very cunning. He secretly painted a whole ceiling panel and put it in place, thus beating all other competitors and winning the commission. In 23 years he produced 50 paintings which completely transformed the inside of the Scuola.

Scuola Grande di San Rocco
Telephone 041 5234864
open every day
9.00 a.m. - 5.00 p.m. (summer)
10.00 a.m. - 4.00 p.m. (winter)

Da Tarcisio
Icecream to satisfy all tastes, pizzas and filled 'calzoni' (folded-up pizza): in between visits it is certainly worthwhile to stop here, just behind the church, for a quick snack.

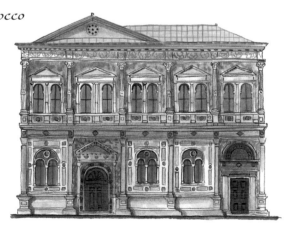

Scuola Grande di San Rocco

The Campo of Santi Giovanni e Paolo

The church of Santi Giovanni e Paolo

This beautiful gothic church, which is called *San Zanipolo* in Venetian (*Zani* and *Polo* are dialect for Giovanni and Paolo), was finished in 1430 for the *Dominicans' Order* and it is the biggest in Venice. Did you know the campo outside the Church was called by the Venetians **Campo delle Maravégie**. Apparently extraordinary things and prodigies happened in this campo of "wonders"; if you do not scare easily, you will find many secrets and weird things in this church. You can start by taking a look at the **Monument to *Marc'Antonio Bragadin.*** The story goes that under the bust of *Bragadin*, who was skinned alive by the Turks in 1571 after the fall of *Famagosta* (the last Venetian citadel on the island of Cyprus), there is an urn which contains his skin! Apart from the **tombs** of other legendary characters such as *Vettor Pisani* and *Sebastiano Venier* (the hero of Lepanto), you will find a relic (a part of a Saint's body!): **St Catherine of Siena's foot.** You will also see the famous **pantheon of the Doges**, funereal monuments and tombs made by *Pietro Lombardo* and other sculptors of the time. Among the 25 doges there is also *Tommaso Mocenigo*, the "Prophet Doge" who, on his death bed, announced the military and economic decadence of the Serenissima if *Francesco Foscari* was to be elected after him. Strangely enough, it all came true. Look carefully at the wonderful paintings kept in the church: the beautiful **polyptych** of *The life of St Vincenzo Ferreri* by *Giovanni Bellini*, the painting of *St. Antonino's alms* by **Lorenzo Lotto** and the **Veronese cycle** in the **Rosary chapel**.

Antico Caffè Rosa Salva

This Café is the right place for fresh orange juice, a toasted sandwich, a house ice-cream or a cake (you should try the cream and raisin pudding). It is in Campo SS. Giovanni and Paolo, on the same spot where one of the oldest cake shops in Venice used to be; in nice weather you can also sit outside.

Pizzeria Alla strega

Witches' hats, broomsticks and cauldrons with boiling potions painted on the walls, this pizzeria with garden offers a very pleasant atmosphere. It is near the church and makes more than 70 different pizzas, to suit all tastes. You can try Halloween pizza, a house speciality with pumpkin sauce.

The statue of Bartolomeo Colleoni

Can you see the statue of the army leader on horseback dominating the campo? It is a work by the Florentine artist *Verrocchio* (*Leonardo da Vinci's* teacher) and it pictures *Bartolomeo Colleoni*, a mercenary leader who left his possessions to the Republic when he died, on condition his statue was put outside San Marco (meaning the Basilica). Personal cults were not allowed by the Serenissima; by tradition, not even the Doge could have a statue in the Piazza.

But the Republic, which needed the money, found a compromise.

Bartolomeo Colleoni had his statue outside San Marco, but it was the *Scuola Grande di San Marco* (where the Venice Hospital is today), next to the *church of the Santi Giovanni e Paolo*, and not the Basilica on the Piazza.

The Venetians were masters of shrewdness!

The church of miracles

Do not fail to see this beautiful little *church of Santa Maria dei Miracoli* built at the end of the 15th century by the architect *Pietro Lombardo*; it really looks like a jewelcase, decorated with precious marble in Renaissance style. ⌐ p. 37 Hidden in a maze of *calli* and *callette*, it rises half from the water and half from the ground, true to the "amphibious" spirit of Venetian architecture.

The name of this church seems to come from the miraculous powers of the **altar piece** (*Virgin and Child*), but also from the fact that it was miraculously built using marble left over from the construction of the *Basilica of San Marco*. ⌐ p. 82-83

Osteria Da Alberto

Sarde in saor, octopus salad, baccalà alla veneziana, tuna croquettes, seafood risotto, spaghetti with "caparosoli"... Friendly atmosphere and an interesting variety of Venetian specialities in this small osteria in Calle Gallina, near the church.

The church of San Pietro di Castello

From via Garibaldi you can reach the *island of San Pietro di Castello*, which was one of the first settlements in Venice. In the church you will see the mysterious **marble throne** which apparently comes from an Arabic tombstone; according to legend, *St. Peter* himself sat on this throne. This island has a magic atmosphere, slightly out of time, maybe also because it has the only grass-covered campo remaining in Venice. The church was the seat of the *Patriarch* of the city and was the *Cathedral of Venice* until 1807, when it was replaced by the *Basilica of San Marco*, which originally was just the Doge's private chapel.  p. 82-83

Once the Venetians used to come to this church on all Lent Sundays and after mass they used to eat *fritole* ↷ p. 59 and the traditional *suca baruca* (roast pumpkin).

Chiesa di San Pietro di Castello
Telephone 041 2750462
open every day
10.00 a.m. – 5.00 p.m.

The Arsenale and the museum of Naval History

Founded in the 12ᵗʰ century and later enlarged, surrounded by tall embattled walls as if it were a city within the city, the Venetian *Arsenale* was the biggest shipyard in the world. It became so famous in the whole of Europe that the word *arsenale*, which comes from the Arabic *darsina'a* (house of industry, activity), soon was used in 14 languages. *Dante Alighieri* himself, seeing the 16 thousand workers of the Arsenale toiling with boiling pitch and tar, was so impressed that he described them in the *21ˢᵗ Chant of the Inferno*. You will see **Dante's bust** on the outer wall near the entrance, where there are also four lions mounting guard. ↷ p. 15

Above the entrance, instead, you will see a **war lion** holding a closed Book of Gospels in its paws. ↷ p. 17

Arsenale
Telephone 041 2709512
Visits can be booked ahead
for small groups
Thursday and Saturday
8.30 a.m. - 12.00 a.m.

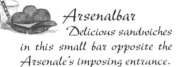

Arsenalbar
Delicious sandwiches in this small bar opposite the Arsenale's imposing entrance.

This huge weapons, oars and naval equipment depot was also the forge where the Venetian war and trade *galleys* were built, maintained and repaired. ↷ p. 133

The Arsenal workers, called *arsenalotti*, worked in teams: carpenters, sawyers, workmen and apprentices all worked like an assembly line, proud to serve the Republic in such a crucial sector for its power and wealth.

If you take the boat at ⬛ **Tana**, you can cross the **Arsenale Vecchio** (which is a military zone, therefore off-limits to the public) and see the wet dock of the shipyards.

If you are interested in knowing more about the ancient splendours of the Venetian fleet, you simply must visit the **museum of Naval History**, near the *Arsenale* and *Riva degli Schiavoni*. There you'll find compasses, naval trophies, firearms, mementos, uniforms, ship parts, maps of fortresses, maritime weapons and a funny device called the "camel", which is a vice that closed around ships and lifted them up just enough for them to be able to float over the shallow waters of the lagoon.

Also on display are some **ship models**, among which a 17th century galleass and the **Bucintoro**, the precious golden galley symbol of the Serenissima which was used to celebrate the *Sensa festival*. p. 111

Museo di storia navale
Castello 2148
Telephone 041 5200276
Closed on Sundays
8.45 a.m. - 1.30 p.m. (from April till June)
8.45 a.m. - 1.00 p.m. Saturdays

 Oddities

Who lived in Campo dei Mori?

Arab merchants who had fled the *Morea* (in the *Peloponnesus*) during the civil war lived in this campo near the *Ghetto* ↷ p. 93 and the *fondamenta della Misericordia*. There are still four **statues** of men from the East wearing turbans on the external walls of the houses, among which the three Moorish brothers *Rioba, Sandi* and *Alfani*, who were silk traders.

How did the Ponte dei Pugni get its name?

The "bridge of fists" is located between *Campo San Barnaba* and *Campo Santa Margherita* ↷ p. 125, where once there used to be clashes between the *Castellani* (inhabitants of the sestieri of Castello, San Marco and Dorsoduro) and *Nicolotti* (from the sestieri of Cannaregio, San Polo and Santa Croce).

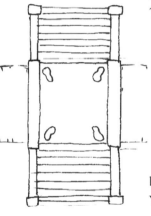

Originally the fighters used rods and then simply their bare hands; since there didn't use to be any railings, they often fell in the canal below. The fights became so violent that they were prohibited in 1705.

You can still see the rival **teams' footprints** on the bridge.

Who was the balotin?

A boy between eight and ten years of age picked at random in the *Basilica of San Marco*, whose task was to extract from the ballot-box the *balote*, cloth balls used for electing the Doge. ↷ p. 89 To be elected to the highest office, at least 25 votes after several votations were required.

If it rains

The Accademia Galleries
The Guggenheim Collection
The museum of 18th century Venice
The museum of Textile and Costume History
The Modern art museum of Ca' Pesaro
The Correr museum
The Querini Stampalia Foundation
The Scuola of San Giorgio degli Schiavoni
Ca' d'Oro and the Franchetti Collection
The Natural History museum

Is it raining today? Don't worry, it's the ideal day to spend indoors. There are a lot of things you can do on a day like this: discover beautiful old and modern paintings; look at the prehistoric remains of dinosaurs or inside an 18th century Venetian palace; discover the treasures of Ca' d'Oro or find out about the legend of St. George and the dragon. Venice hides a thousand secrets and as many surprises!

The Accademia Galleries

The halls of the **Accademia Galleries** hold the most precious and important Venetian paintings. You will find an extraordinary collection of canvases by the most famous Venetian artists of all ages on display here.

Venetian Gothic (14th century): *Paolo Veneziano* and his disciple with the same name *Lorenzo Veneziano,* with their beautiful and refined masterpieces with glimmering golden backdrops (symbol of purity), took inspiration from the first Byzantine icons and the Moorish origin arabesques (the *Virgin's Crowning,* 1325, by Paolo Veneziano).

Lower Renaissance (15th century): *Giovanni Bellini, Vittore Carpaccio* and *Giorgione* introduced in their paintings perspective, the interest in landscape and architecture, the sweet and soft shapes of the figures, who express their feelings through their body postures and facial expressions (*The Legend of St. Orsola,* 1495-1500, by Carpaccio).

Higher Renaissance (16th century): *Titian, Tintoretto, Veronese* and *Lorenzo Lotto* created a special style called *Venetian* in which colour and hue, the play of light and shadow, the paintings' theatricality and the strength of images took on new importance (*Feast in the House of Levi,* 1573, by Veronese).

Baroque and Rococo (17th and 18th century): *Tiepolo, Guardi* and *Longhi* developed a vibrant and refined school of painting, which took a strong interest in the landscape and the life of Venetian society (*The Dance Lesson,* 1741, by Pietro Longhi).

In the **drawings collection** there are also some works by *Leonardo da Vinci* and *Canaletto*'s sketch book. The latter left in his works a nearly photographic rendition of the Venice of his age, the first half of the 1700s.

Gallerie dell'Accademia
Dorsoduro 1050
Telephone 041 5222247
8.15 a.m. - 2.00 p.m. Mondays
8.15 a.m. - 7.00 p.m. from Tuesday to Sundays

The Guggenheim Collection

The palace which holds the Peggy *Guggenheim Collection* was called **Ca' Venier dei Leoni** because apparently the *Venier* family were so extravagant that they kept a lion on a leash! As you will see, construction of the palace never went beyond the first floor, maybe for lack of funds.

The last owner was the wealthy American collector *Peggy Guggenheim*; when she died the palace became a modern art museum open to the public. In its rooms you will find one of the most important **collections of Twentieth century art**: works by *Pablo Picasso, Jackson Pollock, Joan Miro, Piet Mondrian, René Magritte, Wassily Kandinskij, Giorgio De Chirico, Paul Klee* and other famous artists of this century. There is a beautiful **garden** with works by famous sculptors, where you will also see the graves of the eccentric Peggy Guggenheim's many dogs. All their names, from *Leaf* to *Cappuccino* are inscribed on a tombstone. The **gate** is wonderful: it looks like a metal fishing net with bits of colourful glass caught in it.

Peggy Guggenheim Collection
Dorsoduro 701
Telephone 041 2405411
Closed on Tuesdays
10.00 a.m. - 6.00 p.m.
10.00 a.m. - 10.00 p.m. Saturdays in summer
🎫 Salute, Accademia

Gelateria da Nic
You really deserve Nic'
famous gianduiotto: a
irresistible temptation! It's at
the Zattere, near the vaporetti
landing stage

The museum of 18th century Venice

Would you like to know how people used to live in Venice in the 18th century? To find out, you should visit **Ca' Rezzonico**, a real Venetian Baroque palazzo. ↷ p. 37 In the museum you will see **frescoed halls**, paintings, Chinese knick-knacks, mirrors, gilded candelabras, beautiful **Murano glass chandeliers**, **tapestry**, **furniture** which all date back to the 18th century. You will see a **complete bedroom**, but also a **marionette theatre** and an **old pharmacy** of the time. The museum's art collection has paintings by famous Venetian masters of the 18th century, such as *Guardi* and *Tiepolo*. You will see paintings by *Pietro Longhi* as well, which are interesting because they describe exactly the aristocratic atmosphere of the sitting rooms and the Venetians' every day life during his time: the characters, arranged as if on a theatre stage, are caught while busily carrying out their daily activities.

Museum of Ca' Rezzonico
fondamenta Rezzonico 3136
Telephone 041 2410100
Closed on Tuesdays
10.00 a.m. - 6.00 p.m. (summer)
10.00 a.m. - 5.00 p.m. (winter)
🚌 Ca' Rezzonico

Museum of Palazzo Mocenigo
Santa Croce 1992
Telephone 041 721798
Closed on Mondays
10.00 a.m. - 5.00 p.m. (summer)
10.00 a.m. - 4.00 p.m. (winter)
🚌 San Stae

The museum of Textile and Costume History

It has a rich collection of fabrics and books of great historical value and artistic quality. The museum of the palace (a well-kept example of a 17th century Venetian patrician house) has splendid **collections of precious antique and modern textiles**. An interesting selection of **costumes** from different ages is also displayed, as well as clothes and **accessories** documenting 18th century fashion in Venice. There is also an important **library** with approximately 6.000 books specializing in the history of textiles, costume and fashion.

The Modern art museum of Ca' Pesaro

The imposing 17ᵗʰ century **palace of Ca'Pesaro** along the Grand Canal is the venue of a prestigious collection of **modern art paintings and sculptures**. A gem of Venetian Baroque Architecture ↷ p. 37, designed by *Baldassare Longhena*, it hosts works by famous twentieth century Italian artists such as *Boccioni, De Chirico, Sironi* and *Morandi*. There are also many masterpieces by great foreign artists such as *Kandinsky, Chagall, Klee, Matisse, Klimt* and *Mirò*. If you are fascinated by the Ancient Far East, don't miss the precious **collection of Japanese weapons and art** from the *Edo period* (1614-1868), on display on the top floors of the palace.

Museum of Ca' Pesaro
Santa Croce 2076
Telephone 041 5240695
10.00 a.m. - 6.00 p.m. (summer)
10.00 a.m. - 5.00 p.m. (winter)
Closed on Mondays
🏛 San Stae

The Correr museum

It presents an interesting itinerary to discover Venetian history and art. It starts from the **Ala Napoleonica** ↷ p. 81, where *Antonio Canova's* marvellous **statues** are on display, and continues in the rooms devoted to the *Serenissima Republic*. On the second floor there are the **museum of the Risorgimento** and the **pinacoteca**, which also has masterpieces by *Carpaccio* (such as the *Portrait of the Young Man in the Red Beret*), *Bellini* and *Lotto*.

Museo Correr
San Marco 52
Telephone 041 52405211
Open every day
9.00 a.m. - 7.00 p.m. (summer)
9.00 a.m. - 5.00 p.m. (winter)

The Querini Stampalia Foundation

It consists of the estate of the noble *Querini Stampalia* family. The palace (complete with furniture and library) was donated to the city in 1868 by the last descendant. The vast **library** has around 300,000 books. In the **museum-house** you can admire **paintings** by great artists such as *Giovanni Bellini* and *Giambattista Tiepolo*. On the ground floor it is possible to visit the Venetian courtyard turned into a refined **garden** by *Carlo Scarpa*. ↷ p. 41

Fondazione Querini Stampalia
Castello 5252
Telephone 041 2711411
10.00 a.m. - 6.00 p.m.
10.00 a.m. - 10.00 p.m. friday and saturday
Closed on Mondays

The Scuola of San Giorgio degli Schiavoni

Do you know the story of *St. George*? Of how he saved the King's daughter, who was to be sacrificed to a terrible man-eating dragon? What about the story of the little boy called *Trifon*? Of how he freed the Emperor Gordian's daughter from the devil, who had turned into a monster called *Basilisk*? And the miracle performed by the wise *St. Jerome* when he took out a thorn from a fierce lion's paw? The main characters of these legends are three patron Saints of the Dalmatians and their stories are told in the **nine canvases**, called *teleri*, kept in the Scuola, which *Carpaccio* painted between 1502 and 1508, creating a near fairytale atmosphere where even the smallest detail is reproduced with the utmost care. The nine teleri, divided in three *cycles*, were commissioned by the Dalmatians' (called *Schiavoni* at that time) community, who had settled in Venice for commercial reasons and who used to convene in the *Dalmatian Confraternity*.

Scuola di San Giorgio degli Schiavoni
Telephone 041 5228828
9.30 a.m. - 12.30 and 3.30 p.m. - 6.30 p.m. (summer)
9.30 a.m. - 12.30 and 3.00 p.m. - 6.00 p.m. (winter)
Closed on Sundays afternoons and Monday

Ca' d'Oro and the Franchetti collection

It is the only Venetian palazzo that has not been named after its owner, *Marino Contarini*, but after the twinkling gilding which used to decorate its elegant façade, making it glimmer. Completed around 1440 by the *brothers Bon, Ca' d'Oro*, together with Palazzo Ducale ∩ p. 87, is surely the most famous example of Venetian gothic style ∩ p. 36, called *flowered* because of the elegant decorations. Like the *Palazzo Ducale*, the **façade** is embroidered with refined open-work and precious coloured marble, which reveal the profound influence of the Eastern style. Ca' d'Oro holds the **art collection** which belonged to the last owner, *baron Franchetti*, who in 1916 donated it to the State together with the palace. It was thus turned into the present museum, which has recently been restored. Among the most beautiful paintings of the museum there is the **St. Sebastian** (1506) by *Andrea Mantegna*, the marble statue **Young Couple** (1493) by *Tullio Lombardo*, the **Annunciation to the Virgin** (1504) by *Vittore Carpaccio* and **Venus at the Mirror** by *Titian*.

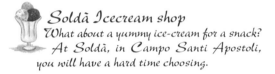

Soldà Icecream shop
What about a yummy ice-cream for a snack?
At Soldà, in Campo Santi Apostoli,
you will have a hard time choosing.

Collezion e Franchetti
Cannaregio 3933
Telephone 041 5238790
Open every day
8.15 a.m. - 7.00 p.m
8.15 a.m. - 2.00 p.m. Monday
🏛 Ca' d'Oro

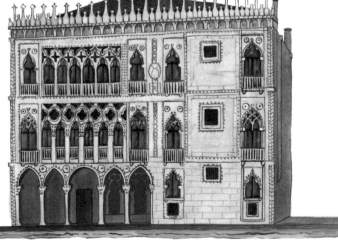

The Natural History museum

Can you see a **dinosaur** in Venice? Yes, in the Natural History museum. It's an *Ouranosaurus Nigeriensis*, a good 7 metres long and 3.6 metres tall. You will also see an ancestor of the crocodile, the *Sarcosuchus Imperator*, as well as a collection of **stuffed animals, minerals, fossils** and a section dedicated to life forms in the lagoon.

The palace, built in Venetian-Byzantine style ↷ p. 36, is one of the most ancient in the city. In 1621 it was bought by the Turks who turned it into a **fondaco** ↷ p. 67 for their trade. After falling into disuse, it was restored under Austrian domination, and became a Natural History museum at the turn of the century.

Museo di storia naturale
Santa Croce 1730
Telephone 041 2750206
9.00 a.m. – 1.00 p.m.
10.00 a.m. – 4.00 p.m. saturday and sunday
Closed on Mondays

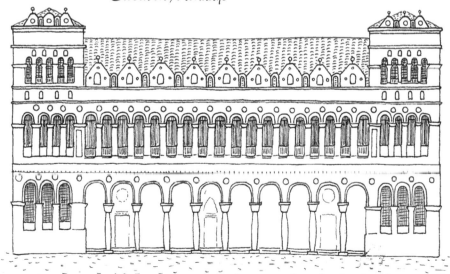

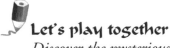

Let's play together

Discover the mysterious object

What is the mysterious object Ciccio is admiring in a drawing room of Ca' Rezzonico? Join the dots to find out.

What did the Festa della Sensa use to celebrate?

On Ascension Day the Doge climbed onto the *Bucintoro*, the stately Doge's galley decorated with friezes and gilding, and threw a *wedding ring* in the lagoon water saying: "We marry you, o sea, as token of effective and perpetual dominion". The Sensa is still celebrated today, but the Doge has been replaced by the mayor in the wedding between Venice and the sea, which used to be the source of all of the Serenissima's power and wealth.

What does the word Carnival mean?

It comes from the Latin *carnem levare* which means abstain from meat. This explains very well the pleasure-loving character of this festival which ends with the beginning of Lent, a time for penitence and renunciation before Easter.

Has the Libro d'oro always contained only noble people's names?

No, to replenish the coffers of the Republic some wealthy merchants were admitted in the book too, provided they disbursed huge sums of money. ⌐ p. 89

What does "bòvolo" mean?

Bòvolo means snail in Venetian; hence the name of the beautiful **Palazzo Contarini** called *del Bòvolo* (1499) (near Campo Manin, behind Campo San Luca) for its peculiarly winding staircase.

What was the Festa delle Marie?

In the *church of Santa Maria Formosa* ⌐ p. 123, every year, on the 30th of January the six sestieri donated a dowry to 12 pretty (but pennyless) girls. The girls were called *The Marys* and they then paraded in sumptuous clothes along the Grand Canal to the *church of San Pietro di Castello*. ⌐ p. 98

The lagoon islands

The Giudecca island
San Giorgio, the cypress island
Lido, Venice's beach
Murano, the island of blown glass
Torcello, the ancient island
Burano, the island of lace

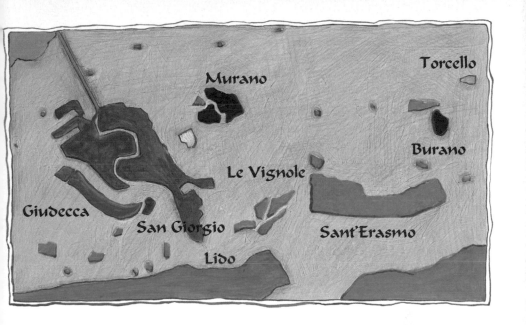

The Giudecca island

In the old times this island was called *Spinalunga* (long fishbone) because of its shape. People used to think the word *Giudecca* referred to the *Jews*, also called *giudei* but it more likely comes from the word *zudegà* (the judged), rebels from noble families who were confined here.

Today the island has lost the majority of its ancient gardens and vegetable patches to make room for new buildings; it has the luxurious **Hotel Cipriani** (the only hotel with a swimming pool in Venice), **Harry's Dolci** (patisserie, bar and restaurant run by *Mr. Cipriani*, the owner of the famous *Harry's Bar* ⌒ p. 147) and the **Zitelle Congress Centre** (in the Palladian **church of the Zitelle**, which has recently been restored), whose name (*zitelle* means spinsters) comes from the fact it used to be a home for unmarried girls who were employed in producing lace. The huge **Stucky mill**, built in *Neo-gothic style* at the end of the 1800's, is under restoration as well.

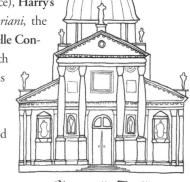

Chiesa delle Zitelle

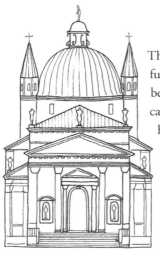

The architectural masterpiece of the island is the beautiful **church of the Redentore**, designed by *Andrea Palladio* between 1577 and 1592, as a token of gratitude when the calamity of the plague ended. Every year the Doge with his retinue visited the church of the Redentore, crossing the Giudecca canal on a **boat bridge**. This was the origin of the **Redentore festival**, which is still celebrated today on the third weekend of July. ⌒ p. 62

Leaving 🚉 San Zaccaria, Zattere
Calling at Giudecca 🚉 Zitelle, Redentore.

Chiesa del Redentore

San Giorgio, the cypress island

Once known as the cypress trees island, it is today the seat of the Cini Foundation, an important cultural centre in which events and conferences are held every year.
The **church of San Giorgio** and the **monastery of the Benedictine friars** were built by the architect *Andrea Palladio* between 1560 and 1580 in Renaissance style, which drew from ancient Rome's classical style. ⌒ p. 37
Inside the church you will find **three paintings** by *Tintoretto*, but the most remarkable piece is the beautiful **St. George and the Dragon** (1516) by *Carpaccio*. The island also has an **open-air theatre**, the *Teatro Verde*. You can take a lift to the top of the bell tower and feel on top of the world at the breathtaking sight of the lagoon.

Leaving 🚉 San Zaccaria (near Piazza San Marco).

Lido, Venice's beach

The *Lido*, which can be reached by *motoscafo* or *vaporetto*, is 12 km long and 1 km wide. It is the only island in the lagoon where there are cars (which arrive from the *Tronchetto island* by *ferry-boat*), and it separates Venice from the Adriatic Sea. In the summer season a visit to the Lido is an interesting alternative to more cultural itineraries and gives you the chance of spending a nice day outdoors.

Leaving 🚢 San Zaccaria (near Piazza San Marco)
Calling at Lido 🚢 S.M. Elisabetta.

The beach

If you fancy a swim, you can walk down the *Gran viale Santa Maria Elisabetta*, the road that cuts across the island from the water-bus landing stage, and you'll get directly to the beach in ten minutes. You will find both the **free beach**, right at the end of the avenue (*Blue Moon terrace*), and many **bathing establishments** where you can rent huts, sun shades, deck chairs or beach beds. The sea is clean and you can swim safely.

Discover the island by bike.

At the beginning of *via Doge Michiel*, right in front of the water-bus landing stage, you can rent bicycles and tandems ∩ p. 156 to go on a nice tour of the island. If you turn left you'll get to the **San Nicolò beach**, the **lighthouse** and the **small Nicelli airfield**. If you turn right, past the *murazzi* ∩ p. 66, you'll get to the small **village of Malamocco** (which in the 8th century was the seat of the lagoon government) and the **Alberoni area** where, in addition to a fine golf course and a fir forest, there's a beach with sand dunes.

Wouldn't it be exciting to go on a sightseeing flight to see the wonders of the Venice lagoon from above? This dream can become reality! At the Nicelli Airfield on the Lido, in the San Nicolò area, there is an Air Club which, as well as flying and parachuting lessons, organizes fantastic sightseeing flights over the lagoon. Ancillotto Air Club Telephone 041 5260808

Murano, the island of blown glass

It is the most densely populated lagoon island and, just like Venice, it is formed by smaller islands connected by bridges.
It is famous all over the world for glassworking.

This traditional craft began in Venice in the 10th century; in 1291 the city's glass makers moved to Murano as a safety measure against the fire hazard.

By the end of the 13th century the island had more than 30,000 inhabitants, with its own government, laws and currency. Between the 15th and the 17th century Murano became Europe's most important glass-making centre. Although they enjoyed remarkable privileges, glass makers could not emigrate without risking severe punishments and sometimes even the death penalty: the craft's secrets had to remain under the Republic's exclusive control.

The ancient splendour of Murano can still be seen in some palaces, but especially in the **Basilica dei Santi Maria e Donato.** This 12th century church is decorated with elegant Venetian-Byzantine columns and beautiful **mosaics**, where exotic birds and mysterious symbols stand out. The most interesting part of the church is the **apse**, covered with a gold-background mosaic of the Madonna.

Leaving from 🚊 Fondamenta Nuove.

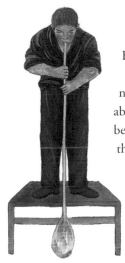

But the island's main tourist attraction is still today the special glass blowing technique of the master glassmakers, who are able to transform a ball of molten glass into beautiful works of art. You can see them at work in one of the island's many glass shops: the demonstration is free.

One of Murano's traditional products are **murrine**, small pieces of cylinder-shaped glass made from coloured glass sticks, molten together to create decorative patterns.

Among the many pieces displayed in the **glass museum**, you will see the famous **Coppa Barovier**: made in blown and enamelled glass, it dates back to the 15ᵗʰ century and is one of the best examples of Murano's refined, traditional production.

Museo vetrario
Glass museum
Telephone 041 739586
10.00 a.m. - 5.00 p.m. (summer)
10.00 a.m. - 4.00 p.m. (winter)
Closed on Wednesdays

Galleria Regina
A pochi passi dal museo, puoi visitare questa famosa galleria che espone le opere di artisti contemporanei del vetro di importanza internazionale.

Torcello, the ancient island

Would you like to sit on **Attila's throne**, the King of the Huns who was also called *God's calamity* because of the cruelty and devastation he brought about?

You will find it in *Torcello*, an enchanted island situated in the heart of Venice's lagoon.

Leaving from 🚤 Fondamenta Nuove; calling at 🚤 Torcello.

Founded by refugees from the roman town of *Altino* in the Venetian inland, fleeing the dangerous barbarians' invasions ↷ p. 18, Torcello once was a prosperous and important island with palaces, churches, convents and more than 10,000 inhabitants.

The ascent and development of Venice caused the island's decline: today only about thirty people live there, and only the **Cathedral of Santa Maria Assunta**, the lagoon's most ancient church, remains to show past glory. Founded in the 7th century, the church holds the great mosaic of the **Last Judgement** and precious carved **bas-reliefs** with images of flowers and animals.

Cattedrale di Santa Maria Assunta
telephone 041 730119
10.30 a.m. – 5.30 p.m. (summer)
10.00 a.m. – 4.30 p.m. (winter)
open every day

Chiesa di Santa Fosca

After the remains of the **Baptistery** and the Byzantine **church of Santa Fosca**, built in the shape of a *greek-cross* (with four equal arms) like San Marco, you can take a look at the **Estuary museum**, where archaeological remains and objects found during the excavations are displayed.

Museo dell' Estuario
Telephone 041 730761
10.30a.m. - 5.30 p.m. (summer)
10.00 a.m. - 4.30 p.m. (winter)
Closed on Mondays

Burano, the island of lace

Sun yellow, geranium red, electric blue, emerald green, fuchsia pink: these are the colours of the houses of *Burano*, which is without doubt the most colourful island of the lagoon.

The **brightly-coloured façades** of painted houses are cheerful, especially on foggy winter days.

Situated in the north of the lagoon, Burano is especially famous for fishing and *lace (merletto* in Italian). In nice weather you might see women sitting outside embroidering their lace with infinite patience and skill.

You can also visit the **Lace school museum** on the island's main square, which is named after *Baldassarre Galuppi*, a famous composer who was born in Burano at the beginning of the 1700s.

Leaving from 🚢 Fondamenta Nuove.

Museo del merletto
piazza Galuppi 187
Telephone 041 730034
10.00 a.m. - 5.00 p.m. (summer)
10.00 a.m. - 4.00 p.m. (winter)
Closed on Tuesdays

 Oddities

What's the renowned "Venetian Blond" (also called Titian blond) for which Serenissima ladies were so famous?

It is a golden, slightly reddish blond hair colour, which can be seen in female figures by great painters such as *Veronese* and *Titian*. Apparently, Venetian ladies used to bleach their hair on the *altane* p. 31, thanks to the combined action of sun light and a special concoction of Damascus soap, alum, horse urine and lead.
Just think what they endured in those times to be beautiful.

What's the Festival del Cinema?

It's an film festival which takes place every year in the first two weeks of September at the **Palazzo del Cinema** on *Lido*. Many Italian and foreign films take part and the best film is awarded the *Leone d'oro*.

What are the Zattere?

The sequence of waterfront walkways along the Giudecca island. The name apparently comes from the word *zattera* (floating lighters) which were used to unload salt, a product Venice had the monopoly over between the 11th and 15th centuries.
Nowadays, especially on fine days, the Zattere is a lively spot where people stroll along and crowd the bars, restaurants and outdoor cafés.

Venice,
a place to play

Where to play and have fun
Games and idioms
Laboratorio Blu and Ludoteca
Playing outdoors
An afternoon at the swimming pool

Where to play and have fun

Where can you play and meet children your age? In Venice there are many **campi** ⌒ p. 29 where children meet to play together. Here's a list of the most important ones, with directions for cafés and ice-cream shops where you can have a snack.

Campo del Ghetto

Campo del Ghetto ⌒ p. 93 has an ancient history, whose traces are still visible today. Nowadays it is mainly a children's playground. Lately, especially in the summer, it has become the kingdom of skaters and roller-bladers, who dash around on the new paving. If you collect telephone cards or similar things, check out the market in September: just before the beginning of school a street fair is held in this campo and on this occasion children organize a **flea market**. Among the old things from people's attics you can find bargains such as comics, magazines, books, collector's items, toys, and lots of other stuff.

Ai Quattro Rusteghi
This café is also a self-service restaurant; it is in the campo and is the ideal place for a sweet or savoury snack.

Campo Santa Maria Formosa

5 minutes from *Piazza San Marco* ⌒ p. 81-85, it is one of the largest *campi*, and a favourite with the locals especially in the afternoon. If you are fond of football (soccer) and handball and love a game, this is the right place for you. You'll find the campo bustling with children cycling, skating, drawing on the ground with chalks, playing with skipping ropes or, when it's hot, having squirt gun battles (a fountain is very conveniently placed in the middle of the campo).

In calle Lunga San Lio nearby there is La Boutique del Gelato which makes one of the best ice-creams in Venice.

In the *Chiesa di Santa Maria Formosa* ↷ p. 111 there are paintings by several famous Venetian painters, in particular a beautiful painting by *Palma il Vecchio* (*Saint Barbara and Saints*, 1510 approx.).

Right in front of the church, in a little house facing the canal, there is the café Zanzibar, *which has a good selection of ice-cream, stuffed rolls, toasted sandwiches, milkshakes and fruit juices.*

Marchini, the confectioner's shop near the Ponte delle Paste (Bridge of Pastries) by Campo Santa Maria Formosa, is famous because all its delicious products are made in its own shop. You will have a hard time choosing among the typical Venetian cookies and cakes.

Campo Santo Stefano

This campo, near the *ponte dell'Accademia* ↷ p. 34, is one of the biggest in Venice. It is famous for the **statue** of the patriot and scholar *Niccolò Tommaseo*, which the Venetians jokingly refer to as *Cagalibri* (a bit rude really, it refers to the position of the books under the writer's bottom). In the old times *bull races* and Carnival balls used to be held here. Nowadays the campo is full of children playing: cycling, skating, skate-boarding, rope and elastic-band skipping, but especially enjoying heated football games against the church wall.

Restaurant-Pizzeria Rosa Rossa
In Calle della Mandola, between Campo Manin and Campo Sant'Angelo, there is a restaurant-pizzeria which offers a good choice of reasonably-priced dishes, as well as a list of pizzas to suit all tastes. A suggestion: try the "pizza Paperino" (Donald Duck's pizza), a speciality of the house with a surprise!

Gelateria Paolin
Snack on the delicious ice-cream from this shop!

Campo Santa Margherita

It is right in the heart of the *Dorsoduro Sestiere* ↶ p. 31 and is always very lively because of the **fruit and vegetable market**, the shops and the busy cafés.

Usually Venetian kids meet here to play football or handball, while little girls play with a *frullo*, a ball tied to a string which is wound around one ankle; you jump over it with the other foot. Children also play team games such as steal the flag or hide and seek, as well as the usual games and activities such as skating, cycling, rope skipping and *campanon* (hopscotch: you draw squares on the ground with a piece of chalk and then you jump on them with one foot).

As it is near the university, the campo has many cafés: try out the take-away pizza from Pizza al Volo, or a sandwich from the Caffè, which is also called Red Bar, and the home-made ice-cream at Causin, with specialities such as "panna in ghiaccio" (an ice-cream sandwich), coffee or chocolate mini-mousses and "moretti" (chocolate-covered ice-cream).

Campo San Polo

This wide campo is the meeting point for soccer players of all ages. Children also ride their bikes, go roller skating and play with the elastic band, which is a complicated game of twisting the elastic around two players' ankles, while a third player must jump over it. In May, just before schools close (in Italy schools close in June), you can hunt for bargains in this campo because there usually is a **children's market** where all sorts of things are for sale: books, comic magazines, toys galore and collectibles such as stickers or telephone cards.

Campo San Giacomo dell'Orio

In the *sestiere di Santa Croce* ⌒ p. 31, near the *San Stae* water-bus landing, you will find this quiet campo with the **Chiesa di San Giacomo dell'Orio** in its middle. One explanation for the campo's name is that it seems to come from the laurel tree (*orio* in Venetian) which once grew near the church. The campo has recently been re-surfaced, much to the children's delight. They gather here to play soccer, skate or cycle, draw with chalks or play "hopscotch".

Cico Bar

It's the ideal place for a break or snack in between games: drinks, fruit juices, toasted sandwiches, ice-cream and popsicles, which Venetian children call "sticks".

Policemen

Since there are no cars, policemen are not as busy in Venice as in other cities. Sometimes they even have time to stop children's games which, because of a strange municipal decree, are not really allowed in Venice (like cycling, skating, roller-blades or soccer: practically everything!).
Luckily, most of the time they are very tolerant. In case they are in a bad mood you'll have nothing left to do but imitate Venetian children, who in these cases just make off with their balls under their arms!

Alaska ice-cream shop

It is definitely worthwhile to pop over to the Campo Nazario Sauro nearby to discover this shop's home-made production of really special ice-creams, which distinguish themselves for their excellent quality and truly creative flavours: besides the classic cream and fruit flavours, you can also try pear, fig, celery, carrot, malt and even corn flake ice-cream!

Games and idioms

Kibacheba

It is a kind of soccer for just two players, so you're centre forward, mid-field and goal keeper all at the same time. To kick the ball you can only go as far as mid-field.

Piera alta

It means *high stone*: someone has to catch all the others, before they climb to safety onto something higher, such as a step.

Mea!

It's Venetian for hide and seek

Ghe!

It's tag you're it.

Ocio!

It means *careful!* and you say it to your football team members, when a ball has been hit especially hard.

Ostrega!

It literally means *oyster*, and it expresses surprise or disappointment.

Laboratorio Blu and Ludoteca

They are two special places where children can play, have fun and meet new friends. Participation in activities is not only for Venetians, but is open to everyone.

Laboratorio Blu

It is a nice bookshop in the *Campo del Ghetto* near the train station and the San Marcuola landing stage.

It specializes in **children's books**. It also organizes all sorts of **workshops**, even several days long: fairy tale reading, pottery, recycled paper, photography, dough figures, juggling etc.

Great Halloween party
On the 31st of October the *Laboratorio Blu* organizes a great *Halloween Party*. A few days before children get together in the bookshop to prepare masks and costumes. It's great fun for everyone!

The Venice Games Library

Are you looking for a place full of games you can use and borrow,
from building bricks to video games? Luckily there is **La Luna nel Pozzo**!
Simply by paying a registration fee you'll get a yearly card and you'll be able to
play with the more than **500 games** available. You can even borrow them and
take them home or to the hotel (for a maximum of 15 days), you only have to
pay a small fee. The card also allows you to participate for free in the many
workshops organized by the Ludoteca: water colours, children's yoga,
origami, marble paper, puppet making etc.

Ludoteca La Luna nel Pozzo
Santa Maria Ausiliatrice
Castello 450
Telephone 041 5204616
14,30-18,30
closet Saturday and Sunday
Giardini

Games, Creativity, Nature

Near the Rialto Bridge and Calle Lunga San Lio, here is a store specialized in games
of all types for a public of all ages. In addition to a well-supplied shelf for juggling
material and educational games for tots, you can also find a vast assortment of
board games. The more curious among you will have a good time with fantastic
brain-teasers, unusual accessories and original curios such as the mystic ball and the
flying top. The interesting science department has articles with
which to observe nature and the environment.

Lanterna Magica
Calle de le Bande
Castello 5379
Giardini

Playing outdoors

Parco Ca' Savorgnan

This park is in *Cannaregio*, between the *Santa Lucia railway station* and the *Ponte delle Guglie*. There are lots of trees, it is clean and well-kept. You can play football, cycle, rope skip, organize toy car races or squirt-gun battles (there obviously is a fountain); you can also have fun with **merry-go-rounds**, **see-saws**, **swings**, a little **wooden house** and even **table-tennis** (you've got to bring your own balls and bats, though).

🚌 San Marcuola, Ponte delle Guglie

Parco
Ca' Savorgnan
8am-6pm (winter)
8am-7pm (summer)

Biennale gardens

For the little ones, in one of the few green areas of the lagoon city, there are many wooden games: little houses, swings, slides, rocking horses, and even a obstacle course and jungle gyms. These gardens are near the **Biennale Art Exhibition's pavilions** ↷ p. 153, and they can be easily reached both on foot (a long and pleasant walk from *Piazza San Marco* along the *Riva degli Schiavoni*), and by boat.

🚌 Giardini

Sant'Elena gardens

Surely the largest public green area in the whole of Venice. The gardens are set in the fine fir forest of the *island of Sant'Elena* (where the **football stadium** is also located) and there are large **picnic areas**, as well as places to play basketball, football, volleyball and to skate. The park has **see-saws**, **slides**, **rocking horses** and other games, which make these gardens suitable for children of all ages, big and small.

🚌 Sant'Elena

An afternoon at the swimming pool

There are two recently-built swimming pools in Venice, where you can swim freely or take courses with an instructor.

Sant'Alvise swimming pool

This swimming pool is not far from the railway station, and it is inside the *Villa Groggia park*, which is also the site of a public library. There are swimming **courses** with an instructor, but at certain times you can also swim on your own if you already know how to.

Piscina Sant'Alvise
Cannaregio 3161
Telephone 041 713567
🚋 Sant'Alvise

Sacca Fisola swimming pool

The modern Sacca Fisola swimming pool is on the island of the same name and can be reached by taking the water-bus across the *Giudecca canal*. The swimming pool organizes fortnightly **courses** of 12 lessons each all year round, except in July and August when it is closed. You can also swim freely by paying an admission ticket. Indispensable gear: bathing suit, cap (obligatory), rubber slippers and bath-robc. The swimming pool has hot water showers and hair dryers, included in the price.

Piscina comunale
Sacca San Biagio island,
Sacca Fisola
Telephone 041 5285430
🚋 Sacca Fisola

131

 # Oddities

What is the Fenice?

The *Fenice* is the phoenix, emblem of the *Teatro La Fenice*. According to legend it is a bird born again from its own ashes. Strange enough, this seems to be the sad destiny of the famous Venetian theatre, which burnt down several times, once on the 12th of December 1836 and, more recently, on the 29th of January 1996.

What was the famous Venetian Ridotto?

It was the first *public gambling house* in Europe, established in 1638 by the *Doge Marco Dandolo*. In this government owned casino, fortunes were blown every evening on gambling and the gamblers had to wear masks in order to be admitted. In 1774 the *Ridotto* was closed down because of the many cases of Venetians who had ended up "in braghe de tela" (cloth trousers, that is, ruined) because of this terrible vice. The gambling mania does not seem to have burnt out in Venice: today there is still the Municipal **Casinò**, *Ca' Vendramin Calergi* ↷ p. 37

How many gondolas are presently being used in Venice?

Around 350, an instrument for a trade that until some time ago was strictly transmitted from father to son, and only recently has been opened, through competition, to all aspiring gondoliers. ↷ p. 43-46

Why is a glass of wine called "ombra" in Venetian?

Because once there used to be a stall selling wine under the *campanile di San Marco*, and the wine was kept cool by the tower's shadow (*ombra* in Italian).

Is there a haunted palace on the Canal Grande?

Yes, **Ca' Dario**, which seems to bring bad luck to its owners, who all died in mysterious circumstances.

Which hotels made the Lido so famous at the turn of the century?

The **Excelsior Hotel**, (which used to be the biggest hotel in the world) with its Moorish-style façade and the **Grand Hotel des Bains** (still beautiful today in its *Art Déco style*), which soon attracted a wealthy and sophisticated international clientele, making the Lido the most famous and fashionable beach in Europe. The characteristic **huts** you can see on the beach are comfortable changing rooms for the bathers.

Is it true that the Arsenale workers could build a galley in 24 hours?

Yes, apparently the *arsenalotti* ⌐ p. 99 were so efficient they could build a warship in just one work day. *Henry III*, King of France, was shown how a Venetian galley had been built and finished while he was partaking of a banquet. Apparently the Serenissima wanted to send him an implicit message about its power and preparedness in case of an attack: he got the picture!

Which famous films have been set in Venice?

INDIANA JONES

Venice, with its unique scenery, is a special and very much sought after film setting. Among the many films that have been set here, **007 Moonraker** with *Roger Moore* and **Indiana Jones and the Last Crusade** with *Harrison Ford* and *Sean Connery*.

Venetian folklore

A few words in venetian dialect
Proverbs and sayings
Songs and rhymes
A venetian fairy tale
A poem about Venice

A few words in venetian dialect

Venetian and Italian are quite different, you know? Below you'll find some commonly used words in Venetian dialect with their Italian and English translation.

Miniature Venetian - Italian - English dictionary

Venetian	Italian	English
Ancùo	*Oggi*	Today
Anelo	*Anello*	Ring
Bala	*Palla*	Ball
Boresso	*Risarella*	Giggles
Botega	*Negozio*	Shop
Caleghei	*Calzolaio*	Cobbler
Ciacolar	*Chiaccherare*	Chat
Ciapar	*Prendere*	Catch
Degheio	*Confusione*	Mess
Famegia	*Famiglia*	Family
Fio	*Ragazzo*	Boy
Fia	*Ragazza*	Girl
Gnanca	*Neanche*	Not even
Imbriago	*Ubriaco*	Drunk
Impissar	*Accendere*	Turn on
Insemenìo	*Sciocco*	Fool
Leon	*Leone*	Lion
Musso	*Asino*	Donkey
Ongia	*Unghia*	Finger nail
Papussa	*Pantofola*	Slipper
Pesse	*Pesce*	Fish
Piron	*Forchetta*	Fork
Poareto	*Poveretto*	Poor
Puteo	*Bambino*	Child
Recia	*Orecchio*	Ear
Satta	*Zampa*	Paw
Scagio	*Ascella*	Armpit
Scarsea	*Tasca*	Pocket
Schei	*Soldi*	Money
Scoasse	*Immondizie*	Garbage
Servelo	*Cervello*	Brain
Sior	*Signore*	Gentleman
Tecia	*Pentola*	Pot
Toco	*Pezzo*	Piece
Tola	*Tavola*	Table
Vecio	*Vecchio*	Old
Verzer	*Aprire*	Open
Vardar	*Guardare*	Look

Proverbs and sayings

Xe più fadiga taser che parlar
It is harder to keep quiet than to talk

Saco vodo non sta drito
An empty sack cannot stand up
(if you don't have enough to eat you won't be strong enough)

A chi no vol far fadighe, el teren ghe produse ortighe
The land only grows nettles if you don't work hard enough
(You've got to work hard in order to earn)

Chi vol star ben, toga le robe come che le vien
If you want to be happy, take things as they come.

El pesse grosso magna el picolo
The big fish eats the small one
(the strongest always wins)

Bronsa coverta
Hidden embers (still waters run deep)
(a person who looks calm and quiet, but in reality is all the opposite.)

I venexiani nasse strachi e vive par riposar
Venetians are born tired and spend their life resting
(a sarcastic comment on the Venetians' laziness)

Xe megio oseo de bosco che de gabia
A bird in the wood is better than a caged one
(Freedom has no price)

Vicentini magnagati, Veronesi tuti mati, Padoani gran dotori, Venexiani gran siori. E de Rovigo? De Rovigo no m'intrigo!
People from Vicenza eat cats, those from Verona are all mad, those from Padua are all great scholars and the Venetians are great lords. And what about Rovigo? I won't meddle with Rovigo!

Songs and rhymes

There are many songs dedicated to Venice, such as *Marieta Monta in Gondola*, *El Vecio Gondolier* or *La Festa del Redentor*. A classical Venetian song, which you will also hear sung by the gondoliers, is *La Biondina in Gondoleta*, which sings of a fair-haired girl taken for a ride on a gondola.

La Biondina in Gondoleta
La biondina in gondoleta
L'altra sera go menà,
Dal piaser la povereta
La s'ha in bota indormenzà.
Una sola bavesela
Sventolava i so caveli
E faceva che dai veli
Sconto el sen no fusse più.
Perchè, oh Dio, che bele cosse
Che go dito e che go fato
No, mai più tanto beato
Ai me zorni non sarò.

The fair girl in the small gondola
The fair-haired girl in the small gondola
The other evening I have taken.
She was so pleased, poor thing,
she suddenly fell asleep.
Just a light breeze
Made her hair flutter
And unveiled her breast.
Why, oh God, what wonderful things
I have said and I have done
No, I will never ever in my life
Be as blissful.

Among the many rhymes, surely *San Martin* is one of the most famous ones. Venetian children sing it on the 11th of November (the day devoted to the Saint) while going from house to house to collect little presents, improvising little concerts with pots and pans. ⌒ p. 63

San Martin

San Martin xe andà in soffita
a trovar ea so novissa.
So novissa no ghe gera
San Martin xe cascà par tera!
E col nostro sachetin
Ve cantaremo el San Martin!

St. Martin has gone up to the attic
To find his fiancée
His fiancée was not there
St. Martin fell down!
And with our little satchel
We will sing you about St. Martin!

Let's play together
A Venetian tongue-twister
Here's a funny tongue-twister in Venetian dialect.
Can you say it?

I ga igà i gai.

It means "They have tied the cockerels",
which in Italian would be "hanno legato i galli".

A Venetian folk tale

The Wild Man

This very old Venetian folk tale tells the story of *Toni* and how he learned to be clever, thanks to the lessons of the *Wild Man*. The **ramo** and **calle del Salvadego** still exist today in Venice near the Post Office, behind *Piazza San Marco*. ↷ p. 81-85

Once upon a time there was a woman who had seven sons; the first six were good boys and hard workers, but the seventh, whose name was Toni, was big and strong but very lazy and all he could think of was food.

One day the woman got angry because Toni had got up to some mischief and chucked him out of the house. Toni wandered aimlessly until, near Piazza San Marco he ran into the Wild Man. He was a big man with a long black moustache and hands like mill blades. His nose was covered in warts and his eyes were as round as two big marbles. When he opened his mouth to speak, it was so big it looked like an oven.

Toni was so frightened he wanted to run away but the Wild Man spoke to him:

– *Where are you running young man, now that your mother has thrown you out of the house? Let's make a deal: you will stay with me as my servant, and I'll make sure you won't regret it. If in one year's time you are not happy, you can go back to your mother and your six brothers.*

Toni was bewildered because the Wild Man seemed to know so many things about him, and even though he was scared to death by the man's appearance, he understood he had no other choice and decided to make the deal.

One year went by and Toni could not complain of the way the Wild Man was treating him: in exchange for his service he received fine clothes, a lodging in the big man's palace right behind Piazza San Marco and as much food as he could eat.

But he was starting to miss his family, so he asked the Wild Man for leave to visit his mother and brothers. The big man agreed and even gave him a present of a donkey saying: – *I beg you, Toni, never tell him to do a poo or there will be an uproar.*

But Toni, being very curious, wanted to try the donkey as soon as he left the Wild Man's palace to see what could ever happen. – *Do-a-poo!* – He told the donkey, and instead of what you might expect, the donkey produced rubies, diamonds and emeralds.

Now, as you might have guessed, the Wild Man was really a very powerful wizard who wanted to test Toni. Overjoyed by his discovery, Toni arrived near the Rialto bridge which was half way to his house. He was a bit tired and it was getting dark, so he decided to stop at an inn. Since, besides being curious he was also a bit of a simpleton, in talking to the inn-keeper he let out – *Please put this magic donkey in a special place because he drops gems instead of poo!*

The inn-keeper, who was on the contrary a very cunning man, made Toni eat and drink as much as he could, and put him to bed snoring like a steam engine. He then crept to the stable to see for himself if what Toni had said was true.

When he saw that if you said *"Do-a-poo!"* the donkey actually made precious gems, he replaced it with a common donkey and kept the magic one.

The next morning, the naive Toni took what he thought was his own donkey and set out for home. When he got there, he couldn't wait to show his mother and brothers the gift the Wild Man had given him.

But he was shocked to see that, when he asked his mother to lay her best sheets, scented with roses and lavender, on the floor, the donkey actually obeyed Toni's order the only way it knew how.

Overwhelmed by the turmoil, the smell and the screams of his mother, who was furious and ready to give him a beating, Toni thought best to slip off.

Crestfallen, he went back to the Wild Man who got terribly angry when he learnt what had happened, and reprimanded him. But eventually he agreed to take him back. After two years, Toni started missing his family again and asked to see them. The Wild Man agreed to let him go and this time gave him a napkin, warning him that he should never say "*Spread out napkin, fold again napkin!*".

Toni, curious as he was, was dying to see what would to happen to the napkin if you gave it that strange order. He had taken just a few steps outside the Wild Man's palace when he pulled out the napkin and said the magic words.

The magic napkin opened out, filling with gold and silver coins and then folded up again, turning into a precious bundle which Toni put in his pocket.

But as soon as he got to the inn at Rialto, the inn-keeper, who, as we know, was very sly, made him eat and drink until Toni was so drunk he told him all about the magic napkin he had in his pocket. The inn-keeper then put him to bed and replaced the Wild Man's napkin, which looked like an ordinary white cotton napkin, with an identical piece of cloth.

Toni, who had hoped to impress his family, had to take to his heels again. His mother and brothers thought he was making fun of them with the story of the magic napkin which was really just an ordinary one, the same as any they had in the house.

Back with the Wild Man, Toni had to endure the reprimands he rightly deserved. He took his place serving again and was good for three years. But at the end of the third year, he again felt a great desire to go back to his family, even though the Wild Man gave him everything he needed and treated him very well. Again the Wild Man agreed to let him go and gave him a present of a club, telling him never to say *"Get up club!"* or *"Get down club!"*

Our Toni was dying to try the club out: he thought for sure it must have some magic power. So as soon as he was far from Piazza San Marco, he pulled the club out of his bag and said – *Get up club!*
He should never have done that! The club started beating him and the more Toni tried to run away, the more it ran after him thrashing him. In the end, breathless and exhausted, he remembered the second order and just managed to whisper – *Get down club!* – Immediately the club slipped back into the bag on its own, and Toni sighed with relief, because he had been afraid it would break his back. All the way to the inn Toni thought about the lesson he had just learned.

Once he got to the Rialto bridge, he let the inn-keeper serve him food and wine, but this time he was careful not to get drunk. Towards the end of dinner he said off-handedly – *You know, this time the Wild Man has given me a magic stick. All you have to do is say "Get up club!" and everything it touches turns into gold. I just can't wait to show it to my family!*

As soon as Toni went to bed and fell asleep, the inn-keeper called his wife and children to get hold of the magic stick and see what wonders it could do. Not content with what he had already stolen from Toni, this time he wanted to roll in riches; his greed seemed endless. But at his command, the club started thrashing all of them. The inn-keeper, his wife and his children tried to run away, but the club was faster and caught up with them, giving them all a thorough beating. Everybody was yelling their heads off and no one knew what to do; in the end the inn-keeper woke Toni up pleading for help.

Toni said – *Of course I can help, but I first want you to return everything you have stolen: the donkey and the magic napkin.*
The inn-keeper, having no other way to make the beating stop, agreed.
So Toni said – *Get down club!* – and the stick slipped back into his bag.
Once he had his treasures back, Toni was able to go home, knowing he was finally going to be welcome.
The magic gifts made the family wealthy, and they moved to a beautiful palace on the Grand Canal.
Thanks to the Wild Man's lesson, Toni learnt to be wiser and less voracious.

A poem about Venice

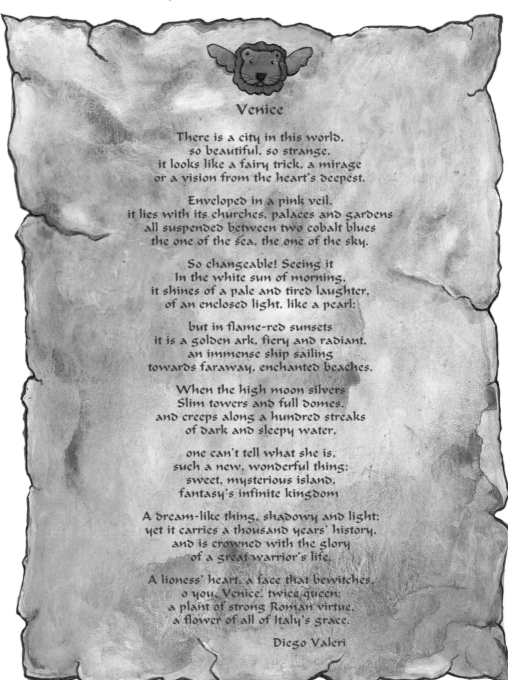

Venice

There is a city in this world,
so beautiful, so strange,
it looks like a fairy trick, a mirage
or a vision from the heart's deepest.

Enveloped in a pink veil,
it lies with its churches, palaces and gardens
all suspended between two cobalt blues
the one of the sea, the one of the sky.

So changeable! Seeing it
In the white sun of morning,
it shines of a pale and tired laughter,
of an enclosed light, like a pearl:

but in flame-red sunsets
it is a golden ark, fiery and radiant,
an immense ship sailing
towards faraway, enchanted beaches.

When the high moon silvers
Slim towers and full domes,
and creeps along a hundred streaks
of dark and sleepy water,

one can't tell what she is,
such a new, wonderful thing:
sweet, mysterious island,
fantasy's infinite kingdom

A dream-like thing, shadowy and light:
yet it carries a thousand years' history,
and is crowned with the glory
of a great warrior's life.

A lioness' heart, a face that bewitches,
o you, Venice, twice queen:
a plant of strong Roman virtue,
a flower of all of Italy's grace.

Diego Valeri

Venice

C'è una città di questo mondo,
ma così bella, ma così strana,
che pare un gioco di fata morgana
o una visione del cuore profondo.

Avviluppata in un roseo velo,
sta con sue chiese, palazzi, giardini,
tutta sospesa tra due turchini,
quello del mare, quello del cielo.

Così mutevole! A vederla
nella mattina di sole bianco,
splende d'un riso pallido e stanco,
d'un chiuso lume, come la perla:

ma nei tramonti rossi affocati
è un'arca d'oro, ardente, raggiante,
nave immensa veleggiante
a lontani lidi incantati.

Quando la luna alta inargenta
torri snelle e cupole piene,
e serpeggia per cento vene
d'acqua cupa e sonnolenta,

non si può dire quel ch'ella sia,
tanto è nuova mirabile cosa:
isola dolce, misteriosa,
regno infinito di fantasia...

Cosa di sogno, vaga e leggera;
eppure porta mill'anni di storia,
e si corona della gloria
d'una grande vita guerriera.

Cuor di leonessa, viso che ammalia,
o tu, Venezia, due volte sovrana:
pianta di forte virtù romana,
fiore di tutta la grazia d'Italia.

Diego Valeri

 # Oddities

What is Harry's Bar?

It's a famous bar and restaurant near Piazza San Marco, which is a favourite haunt of Americans (it was the American writer *Ernest Hemingway*'s favourite bar). The owner, *Arrigo Cipriani*, has invented a famous speciality, the **Bellini cocktail**, which is sparkly wine mixed with white peach juice. ⌐ p. 113

What are barbacani and mascheroni?

Barbacani are cantilevered wooden structures built under the second floor of houses, which increase the surface of the house without invading the calle.
Mascheroni are men's heads or grotesque figures carved in stone, used as decorations on the façades of palaces.

Why is there the bust of an old lady with a mortar at the bottom of the Mercerie, near the Torre dell'Orologio?

It is in memory of something funny that happened in 1310, during the conspiracy led by *Bajamonte Tiepolo* and *Marco Querini*.
The conspiracy failed because an old lady, hearing a noise in the calle, leaned out of the window and dropped her mortar (which was once used to grind salt and spices) by accident, hitting the rebels' flag bearer right on his head and killing him. In gratitude the Republic allowed the old lady to stay in her house without paying rent and dedicated the stone bust to her.

Holiday scrapbook

My favourite photo
My notes
My drawing of Venice: I see it like this
My top sights chart

My favourite photo

Stick the photo of the sight you liked most in Venice on the door on this page.

My notes

Thoughts, notes… anything you want!
Here you can write everything that particularly impressed you about Venice.

My drawing of Venice: this is how I see it

Have you got crayons and felt-tip pens? This page is dedicated to drawing "your" Venice, to how you see this city suspended between sky and water.

My top sights chart

After each visit, make a hit list of the things you liked most. In this chart, give a mark in stars:

⭐ = mmhh… so so   ⭐ ⭐ = good   ⭐ ⭐ ⭐ = wow, super!!!

Oddities

What does the weather vane on the Punta della Dogana, near the church of La Salute represent?

The goddess of Fortune, standing on the earth's golden globe, supported by two bronze giants called Atlantes.

What is the Biennale?

The *Biennale of Contemporary Art* is an international exhibition taking place every two years in the pavilions near the Castello gardens. The most interesting works of artists from all continents are shown at the *Visual Arts Biennale*, whereas the most significant plans, photos and models by the most important architects in the world are displayed at the *Architecture Biennale*.

What are the Venetian nizioletti?

> PISCINA DE FREZZARIA

They are road signs painted on the outside walls of houses indicating the name of the *calle, fondamenta, salizada, piscina, corte, riva, campo, ramo, sestiere, rio terà* or *sottoportego*. ⌐ p. 29-31 Nizioletto means little bed sheet: apparently the names were originally written on pieces of white cloth that looked like small bed sheets.

What does popular folklore say about the noble Labia family?

They say it was one of the wealthiest families in Venice. It is said that *Gian Francesco Labia*, at the end of a banquet to which many Venetian noble families had been invited, threw gold plates and silverware in the canal saying: "L'abia o non l'abia, sempre Labia!" (Whether I have it or not, I will always be a Labia, which in Italian sounds like 'Have-it'!).

The **Palazzo Labia**, which is between the Railway Station and the *Ponte delle Guglie*, today houses the seat of the *RAI* (Italian Broadcasting Corporation).

Useful addresses

For general tourist information

Apt Venezia

Central information number 041 5298711
Office in the **Santa Lucia railway station**   *telephone 041 5298727*
Headquarters in **Piazzale Roma** (inside the City garage)   *telephone 041 5298746*
Villa Franchin, Viale Garibaldi 155, Mestre   *telephone 041 5346268*
"**Venice Pavillion**" (near Harry's Bar)   *telephone 041 5225150*
Office in **Lido**, viale S.M. Elisabetta 6   *telephone 041 5265721*
Office in the **Marco Polo airport** at Tessera (arrivals)   *telephone 041 5415887*

Informagiovani – youth information services

Villa Franchin, Viale Garibaldi 155, Mestre   *telephone 041 5346268*
For free information and advice on tourism, vacations, school and work. In our office you will find a library with a wide selection of magazines for young people and a bulletin board for messages and information on events.

Cts – Student travel services

Dorsoduro *3252* (near Ca' Foscari), San Marco 1529   *telephone 041 5205660*
For all kinds of information on travel opportunities in Italy and abroad with special rates for young people and students.

Guided Tour Reservation Center

Association of Tour Guides   San Marco 750   *telephone 041 5209038*
Guided tours of the five Synagogues and Hebrew art museum   *telephone 041 715359*

Rolling Venice and Carta Giovani

These are membership cards which guarantee discounts on the cost of public transportation, or tickets to movies, museums, exhibits, events and allow you to get discounts in many stores all around the city.
Rolling Venice can be acquired at any "Vela" stand of the ACTV;
Carta giovani can be had at Informagiovani.

Internet websites

www.virtualvenice.net
www.turismovenezia.it
www.alata.it
www.venetia.it

To move around the city

Public Transportation

Public transportation in the city is provided by the ACTV ⌢ p. 49
It is advisable to buy ACTV tickets before going on board or else you
will have to pay a surcharge. The ordinary ticket is one way, but it is
also possible to buy a **Day ticket** (valid 24 hours) or the **Three-day
pass**. Veneto residents can ask for **Carta Venezia** with a three-year valid-
ity, to obtain reduced fares. Between Venice and the mainland, transportation is provided by the ACTV's **orange buses** or the ATVO's **blue
buses**, leaving from piazzale Roma.
ACTV information "VELA Call-Center" *telephone 041 2424*
ATVO information *Central information number 041 383671*

Gondole-traghetto on the Canal Grande

San Marcuola-Fondaco dei Turchi *8–13 (except Sundays and holidays)*
Santa Sofia-Pescheria *7–20,55 (Sundays and holidays 7,30–18,55)*
San Silvestro-Riva del Carbon *8–14 (except Sundays and holidays)*
San Tomà-Ca' Garzoni *7–20,55 (Sundays and holidays 8–19,55)*
San Samuele-Ca' Rezzonico *8–13,15 (except Sundays and holidays)*
Santa Maria del Giglio-La Salute *7–20,55 (winter 8–18)*

For your free time

Net House – Internet Café

San Marco 2967-2958 telephone 041-2771190 (open every day 9 a.m.–2 a.m.)
Need to connect on the web or print your digital photos? Just two steps away from the
Santa Lucia Train Station you will find an Internet Point with modern technological
workstations to surf the Web at high speed, assisted by our qualified personnel.
You will find a variety of services such as sending and receiving faxes, a Web Cam,
printing for digital media, CD burning and scanning.
There are also many software and hardware articles on sale and make international
telephone calls. There are discounts and special rates for students.

Bike rentals

Giorgio Barbieri, *via Zara 5, Lido di Venezia telephone 041 5261490*

To buy

Alberto Valese - marble paper
San Marco 3471

In his workshop, Alberto Valese hand paints paper and silk with the marbling technique, an ancient traditional system of Japanese origin, which was brought to Europe by the Turks in the Middle Ages. In his shop, between Campo Santo Stefano and Campo Sant'Angelo he has silk scarves and ties, and many paper items such as notebooks, telephone books, pencil holders, files and photo albums, all in beautiful hues and patterns.

Papier Maché
Castello 5175

Would you like to see how a mask is made? Here's a really special address: in Calle Lunga Santa Maria Formosa (near Campo Santa Maria Formosa) you can visit this craftman's workshop where the different phases of making a mask will be explained and shown to you, from making the papier maché to the final decoration. It is a shop, too, where you can buy all kinds of beautiful masks.

Mondonovo
Dorsoduro 3063

Who would you like to be for a day? Sherlock Holmes or Tutankhamen? Cristoforo Colombo or Pinocchio? The choice is difficult at Mondonovo, near Campo Santa Margherita, which has its own workshop of beautiful handmade masks. They are made in papier maché with extremely accurate details, and faithfully reproduce characters from all ages; display them on the wall when Carnival is over.

Top One
San Polo 2718

If you'd like to buy a present or a souvenir of Venice, don't forget traditional Murano glass. In this shop near Campo San Polo you will find plenty of glass objects to suit every purse: animal families, pendants, earrings, bangles, scent bottles, saucers, photo frames, pill boxes and paper weights. The glass is either blown or lamp-worked, and it is often decorated with "murrine".

Molin giocattoli
Cannaregio 5899
If you are looking for a nice toy shop in Venice, you'll find it near Campo Santi Apostoli: it is on the Ponte San Giovanni Crisostomo, which the Venetians call Ponte dei Giocattoli (Bridge of Toys). Browsing in it you will find toys for all ages and all pockets. Micromachines, transformers, models, board games, mechanical and remote-controlled toys, monsters, stuffed animals, all kinds of dolls with dresses and accessories, jigsaw puzzles, inflatable globes, juggler's items, magic tricks, building bricks and the latest new toys.

Emporio Pettenello
Dorsoduro 2978
This old store in Campo Santa Margherita dates back to 1889: a tradition of more than 100 years in the business, which make it Toy Paradise. The atmosphere is still that of olden times, although there are also a wide range of modern toys. The items on the old shelves can satisfy any taste: kaleidoscopes, music boxes, tin cars, dolls' house furniture, educational games, all kinds of jigsaw puzzles, globes, board games, miniature and clockwork animals, yo-yos, reproductions of antique toys and much more.

Il Baule Blu – antique toys
San Polo 2916
What were your parents' or grandparents' favourite toys? To find out, check out this unusual shop in Campo San Tomà where, in addition to all kinds of plush animals in all sizes (even man-sized), you will find a wide choice of antique toys, restored with patience and skill by the two ladies who own the shop. The shop specializes in plush toys – especially teddy bears – from the turn of the century to the 1950s, but there are also wooden toys, china or celluloid dolls, puppets and everything from the good old days.

Swatch Store
San Marco 4947
Between Rialto and San Marco, this shop is a temple for all fans of the famous Swiss watches. Collections of mad, bizarre and eccentric watches, but also classical, sports, ultra-thin, as well as watches designed by famous artists: in a world of fantastic ideas you'll surely find the swatch that suits you. As well as alarm clocks, answering machines, twinphones and cordless phones, there are the Flik-Flak watches, made especially for children. Time is what you make of it.

Testolini
San Marco 1744

Behind Piazza San Marco, not far from the Bacino Orseolo, Testolini has a decidedly outstanding space and selection compared to the rest of Venice. The stationery and art department is very well stocked; it also sells gifts, office supplies and software.

Disney Store
San Marco 5257

It is in Campo San Bartolomeo, right at the foot of the Rialto bridge. With a giant TV screen showing Disney movie and cartoon characters running non-stop in the background, you can browse through the many items on sale: watches, stationery, videos, stuffed animals, gadgets, as well as bath and home accessories. Don't forget to check out the many different things to wear for Mickey Mouse and Donald Duck lovers.

Cacao
Cannaregio 5583

Lively and colourful children's clothing in Campo Corner, between Campo San Bartolomeo and Campo Santi Apostoli. For every season new sport lines or more elegant clothes, with various accessories.

D.M. Venezia
San Marco 5545

If you are a fan of magicians, unicorns, fairies, elves and knights or you love Magic, Warhammer, Star Trek and Dungeons and Dragons cards, this store just two steps away from the Rialto Bridge is heaven! In addition to the classic painted historic soldiers and miniatures for collectors, you will also find a variety of board games, models, Action Figures, entire armies for War Games and all the latest in the Fantasy department. There is also an interesting section of instruction manuals for role games and a wide selection of Japanese manga comics. There are beautiful historical chessboards with the Crusader and Sarazin armies facing one another, or Napoleon's army against the English troops at the Battle of Waterloo.

Useful numbers

Carabinieri	112
Police	113
Fire Brigade	115
ACI Car Breakdowns	116
Ambulances	118
Hospital emergency room	041 5294517
Emergency veterinary services	041 5294111
Local Police Venezia	041 2747070
Local Police Piazzale Roma	041 5224576
Local Police Venezia Lido	041 5260395
Harbour Office	041 2405711
Actv information: VELA Call-Center	041 2424
ACTV Lost Property	041 2722179
Taxis and Motorboat	041 5222303
Gondola service	041 5285075
Railway Information	892021
Train Customer Assistance	041 785670
Railway Lost Property	041 785238
Airport Information Office	041 2609260
Airport Lost Property	041 2609222
APT claim desk	041 5298710
Municipality Information Office	041 2748080
Tourist Information Office	041 5298711
Tourist Guides Association	041 5209038
"Churches of Venice" Information Office	041 2750462
"Informalmente"	041 2759555
Youth hostel Fondamenta Zittelle	041 5238211
Youth hostel Santa Fosca	041 715775
Toll-free hotel reservations	800 843006
Accademia Cinema	041 5287706
Cinema Lido	041 5265736

Index
of names

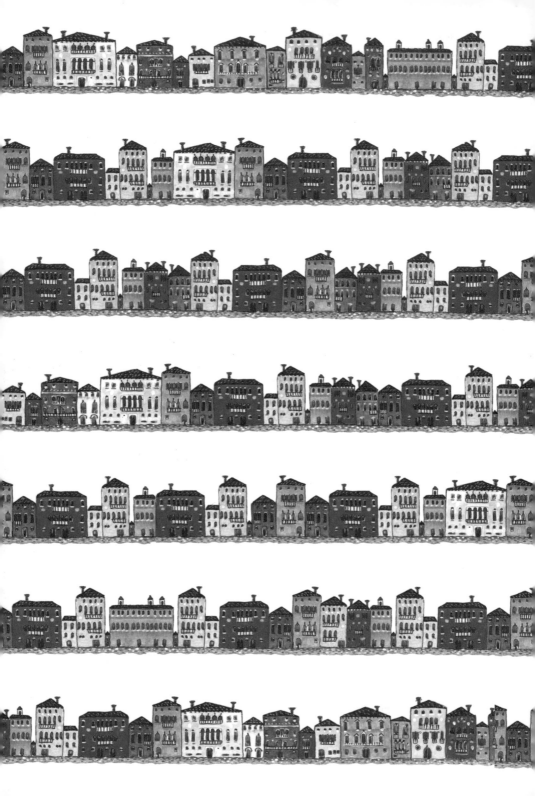